1 Introduction

The recent financial crisis has underscored the complex relationship between the credit risks and liquidity provisions of major financial intermediaries (Bernanke, 2009; Brunnermeier, 2009). In particular, deterioration in the balance sheets of these institutions, caused by declining asset prices and increasing capital charges, severely limited their ability and willingness to provide liquidity. In turn, the liquidity freeze accelerated the decline in asset prices and aggravated the distress of these financial intermediaries. This vicious cycle was exacerbated by surging investor demand for liquidity during a general crisis of confidence.

In this paper, we study the fragility of liquidity during systemic events. We focus on discretionary liquidity provision, where a financial intermediary is only implicitly assumed, rather than legally obligated, to provide liquidity to investors. Such an implicit feature is common in financial contracting (Boot, Greenbaum and Thakor, 1993; Gorton and Souleles, 2006). Indeed, some markets with these types of implicit contracts—for example, the markets for some asset-backed commercial paper and structured investment vehicles—have been at the center of the recent crisis (Acharya, Schnabl and Suarez, 2010). Theorists suggest that discretionary liquidity support may be viable when a financial intermediary values its reputation. But when the liquidity provider is hit by negative shocks in other parts of its balance sheets, it may forfeit its reputational capital by stopping funding projects or making markets, even if these projects or markets are fundamentally sound (Boot et al., 1993; Brunnermeier and Pedersen, 2009; Detragiache, Garella and Guiso, 2000; Gorton and Souleles, 2006; MacLeod, 2007). Empirically, however, the implications of discretionary liquidity provision for market stability and systemic risks are not well understood, in part because most existing studies focus on financial fragility caused mainly by investors' run for liquidity when liquidity provisions are legally binding.[1]

We try to bridge the gap by providing empirical evidence on the dynamics of the fragility of discretionary liquidity provision and analyzing empirically its economic consequences. The laboratory of our study is the recent collapse of the market for auction rate securities (ARS). ARS are long-term bonds or preferred stocks whose interest rates or dividend yields are periodically reset through auctions. Until its collapse, the ARS market had been an important and growing source of funds for municipalities, student loan authorities, and

---

[1]For example, a large body of the literature has studied runs in the demand deposit markets where banks are contractually bound to meet withdrawal requests. See, e.g., Diamond and Dybvig, 1983, Gorton, 1988, Calomiris and Kahn, 1991, Diamond and Rajan, 2001, and De Bandt and Hartmann, 2002. During the recent financial crisis, various markets also experienced such bank run-type disruptions. See, e.g., Covitz, Liang and Suarez (2009) on the asset-backed commercial paper market, Gorton and Metrick (2009) on the repurchase agreements market, and (Shin, 2009) on commercial banking.

closed-end mutual funds.[2] Meanwhile, it was widely used by corporate treasurers and wealthy individuals as a cash-equivalent investment (Austin, 2008; Comment, 2010). For ARS to function as liquid investment vehicles, auction dealers—mostly major broker-dealers—may be needed to bid on their own accounts to help clear the auctions. However, such liquidity provision is discretionary because it is not explicitly stipulated in the debt contract.

The ARS market collapsed in mid-February 2008, with the rate of auction failures shooting up to about 85 percent. Before that, ARS auctions had rarely failed (Austin, 2008). As auctions failed en masse, ARS lost their appeal as cash-equivalent investment vehicles, and their interest rates skyrocketed. In addition, the issuance of ARS has yet to restart.

To examine the dynamic role of auction dealers during this episode, we construct a comprehensive dataset using both auction results and intraday transactions data on ARS issued by municipalities, or MARS. We focus on MARS because we have transactions data for this market segment. In addition, MARS accounted for roughly one-half of the overall ARS market by the end of 2007.

Our main findings are the following. First, we provide quantitative evidence that auction dealers effectively acted as "market makers" before the crisis in mid-February 2008. Auction dealers had routinely bid on their own accounts to absorb surplus supplies of ARS in auctions. Specifically, on a typical auction day, more than one-half of the auctions did not have enough bids from investors, and auction dealers would purchase on their own accounts more than 40 percent of the dollar amount of MARS sold by investors. More strikingly, in nearly one-fourth of the auctions, investors made no bids at all. That is, dealers were not only the bidders of last resort but also the only bidders in these auctions. Meanwhile, like market makers, auction dealers managed their inventories by selling in the non-auction secondary market those bonds acquired from previous auctions. Importantly, dealers' own bids in auctions are not easily observable due to the lack of market transparency. Our in-depth analysis of these market dynamics contributes to the scant literature on the ARS market.[3]

Second, we find that market-making by auction dealers significantly affected both net investor demand and auction clearing rates. In the pre-crisis period, bond fundamentals and auction design explain only a small fraction of the variation in the likelihood of investor demand shortfall—a situation in which investor bid orders are not sufficient to cover all investor sell orders. This finding suggests that, when dealers were making the market,

---

[2]According to data from Thomson Reuters, over the five years from 2003 through 2007, ARS accounted for about 10 percent of the total gross issuance of long-term municipal bonds.

[3] There exist only a few studies on ARS, mostly based on limited data on auction rate preferred stocks. See, Alderson, Brown and Lummer (1987), Winkler and Flanigan (1991), and Alderson and Fraser (1993). As an exception to these studies, McConnell and Saretto (2010) examine the pricing of auction rate bonds. We will discuss this study later.

net investor demand was driven largely by exogenous liquidity demand. In contrast, in the post-crisis period, without auction dealers' support, net investor demand in auctions was strongly related to bond fundamental values and auction design. In particular, the likelihood of investor demand shortfall was strongly and negatively related to the maximum auction rate—the reset rate that is stipulated in the debt contract and applied when an auction fails. All else being equal, the likelihood of investor demand shortfall decreases 17 percentage points for an increase of 1 standard deviation in the maximum auction rate (about 4 percentage points). This result suggests that without auction dealers committing to make markets, investors are more willing to bid for ARS that pay higher interest rates in failed auctions to compensate for the lack of liquidity.

For auction clearing rates, we find that in the pre-crisis period, when auction dealers supported the auctions, they were fairly close to other comparable short-term municipal bond rates. In addition, the rates were strongly related to fundamental bond values but not to maximum auction rates. In contrast, in the post-crisis period, auction clearing rates were only weakly related to bond fundamentals but strongly and positively related to maximum auction rates. These findings are consistent with the predictions of auction theories. In particular, theories show that in the pre-crisis period, when the supply in the auction can be endogenously adjusted, the auction clearing rate approaches the competitive equilibrium level (see, e.g., Back and Zender, 1993). But without liquidity support, as in the post-crisis period, uniform-price auctions may have multiple equilibria; the one preferred by investors has a clearing rate that is arbitrarily close to the maximum auction rate (see, e.g., Wilson, 1979; Back and Zender, 1993).

Our results provide a very different perspective from McConnell and Saretto (2010), who also examine the recent ARS market collapse. In contrast to our study, they do not consider the role of auction dealers in clearing auctions and determining reset rates. In addition, because they pooled data from before and after the market collapse, their analysis may be subject to model misspecification issues. They cannot explain why bonds with lower risk of auction failures—those with higher maximum auction rates—had higher auction reset rates. Our analysis shows that, once we take into account the dealers' role as liquidity providers, this seemly puzzling relationship may be easily understood within the framework of existing auction theories. Our results echo previous findings that broker-dealers exercise substantial impacts on the dynamics and asset prices in the opaque markets such as those for municipal bonds and corporate bonds (Green, Hollifield and Schurhoff, 2007a; Green, Hollifield and Schurhoff, 2007b; Goldstein and Hotchkiss, 2007).

Our third main finding is that implicit liquidity support is fragile during systemic events and reputational externality among major auction dealers exacerbates that fragility. The theory of implicit contracts suggests that when the party assuming the implicit obligation is concerned about its survival, it will forfeit its reputational capital to preserve financial capital (Boot et al., 1993; Gorton and Souleles, 2006). We show that, indeed, before they stopped supporting the auctions, auction dealers were under severe inventory stress and found themselves in a capital crunch. Major auction dealers pared down their ARS inventories in 2007, but their inventories shot up dramatically in early 2008. Meanwhile, turmoil in other financial markets caused substantial deterioration in the overall balance sheets of major dealers. As a result, the riskiness of major auction dealers' liabilities, measured by their credit default swap (CDS) premiums, rose sharply around the same time as did their ARS inventories.

We also find additional evidence that auction dealers traded off between their own financial health and their implicit obligations in providing auction liquidity. Specifically, in the pre-crisis period, the reset rates of those auctions with dealers' supporting bids rise with dealers' funding costs. That is, auction dealers required additional interest rates to compensate for their costs of market-making activities.[4]

Moreover, we show that major auction dealers withdrew suddenly as a group, after an unexpected first-mover stopped making markets. We also find that, the first dealer that completely withdrew its liquidity support had only a below-average level of funding pressure, measured by market share, inventory, and funding cost. These findings suggests that the provision of implicit liquidity support may be unstable during systemic events.

The rest of the paper is organized as follows: Section 2 briefly introduces ARS and documents the recent collapse of the ARS market. Section 3 describes our data and sample statistics. Section 4 provides empirical evidence on auction dealers' role as market makers, their effect on investor demand and auction clearing rates, and the fragility of discretionary liquidity support during systemic events. Finally, section 5 concludes and discusses the policy implications of our research.

2 ARS and the Collapse of the ARS Market

2.1 What Are ARS?

ARS are long-term bonds or preferred stocks with interest rates or dividend yields periodically reset through Dutch auctions, typically every 7, 28, or 35 days. Historically, ARS were mostly issued by municipalities or their authorities in the form of tax-exempt or taxable

---

[4]This result is also consistent with previous findings that in the equity markets, market makers' inventory costs and profitability affect liquidity provision (see, e.g., Comerton-Forde, Hendershott, Jones, Moulton and Seasholes (2010)).

bonds (municipal ARS, or MARS), by corporations or closed-end mutual funds in the form of preferred stocks (ARPS), or by student loan authorities (student loan ARS, or SLARS). The investors were typically corporate treasuries and high-net-worth individuals looking for liquid securities yielding more than money market funds or other cash accounts.[5] In terms of size, the ARS market was substantial: ARS outstanding totaled about $330 billion at the end of 2007, roughly one-half of which was accounted for by MARS.

When auctions are successful, ARS tend to be priced like short-term securities as investors may easily liquidate their positions. Thus, ARS effectively transform long-term liabilities into short-term debt. This maturity transformation is particularly attractive to municipal bond issuers because of the generally steeper yield curve for municipal bonds (Green, 1993) and the limitations on municipalities in issuing short-term debt.[6] As shown in Figure 1, MARS issuance soared from 2002 to 2004, when the municipal term spread, the difference between long- and short-term municipal bond interest rates, was persistently wide, making the maturity transformation particularly favorable at least in the short run. However, MARS issuance decreased somewhat over the next few years as the term spread fell, and then came to an abrupt halt after December 2007, even as the term spread rose sharply.[7]

2.2 The Auction Process

As mentioned above, the ARS auction serves two purposes: setting the interest rate for the period before the next auction (price discovery) and facilitating the transfer of ownership (liquidity). As illustrated in Figure 2, in the auction, existing bond owners submit sell orders and potential investors submit buy orders through auction dealers.[8] Auction dealers, often the securities underwriters, observe all the orders and, at their discretion, place their own orders into the auctions.

---

[5]Comment (2010) finds that, as of December 2007, 645 nonfinancial firms had ARS holdings, with a total of about $40 billion, or 28 percent of the typical company's holdings of cash, cash equivalents, and short-term investments.

[6]State and local governments are generally prohibited by law from issuing short-term debt to finance long-term projects. The two main types of short-term debt are tax anticipation notes and revenue anticipation notes—debts issued in anticipation of, respectively, the collection of future taxes and revenues (usually intergovernmental aid). These debts have to be repaid within one calendar year.

[7]Similar data on ARPS issuance are not available. However, Alderson and Fraser (1993) suggest that after rapid growth, ARPS contracted substantially in the early 1990s, when concerns over corporate credit quality caused a steep rise in auction reset rates.

[8]Existing bond owners may place three types of orders: (a) a hold order, the par amount of the securities they wish to continue to hold, regardless of the clearing rate; (b) a limit sell or "hold at rate" order, the par amount of securities they will hold as long as the clearing rate is no lower than a specified rate; and (c) a market sell order, the par amount of securities they wish to sell irrespective of the clearing rate. Potential investors may place only limit buy orders, in which they specify the par amount of the securities they wish to buy if the clearing rate is no lower than a specified rate.

After all orders, including those from both investors and auction dealers themselves, are gathered, sell and buy orders are ranked by rate. Bids with successively higher rates are accepted until all the securities being auctioned are sold. When the total amount of bid orders is greater than the amount of sell orders, the clearing rate is the lowest rate at which bids are sufficient to cover all the sells. As in a typical uniform-price auction, the clearing rate applies to all winning bids. Multiple bids at the clearing rate are filled on a pro rata basis.[9]

If the total bid orders from investors and auction dealers are not sufficient to cover all sell orders, the auction fails to clear. In this case, interest rates are reset at maximum auction rates determined by the rules specified in the bond prospectus, and sell orders are filled pro rata. Sellers with unfilled orders are compensated by generally high maximum auction rates for the illiquidity.[10]

2.3   The Role of Auction Dealers

Because auction dealers observe investor orders before their own discretionary bids, they can potentially dictate auction outcomes. In particular, when not all investor sell orders can be filled, an investor demand shortfall (IDS) occurs. In this case, if dealers do nothing, the auction fails, current investors must hold the unsold securities until the next auction, and the issuer pays the maximum auction rate. We refer to this situation as an "actual failure." If, however, dealers step in with sufficient backstop bids, the auction will appear successful. For ease of exposition, we refer to this event as a "pseudo failure."

Importantly, unlike actual failures, pseudo failures are not easily observable because they are not disclosed. Major dealers do warn their clients about the liquidity risk in a generic manner in bond prospectuses. Specifically, the prospectus may include language like, "Dealers *may* (routinely) bid in the auctions on their own accounts but are not obligated to do so."[11]

---

[9]If all existing bondholders decide to retain their holdings irrespective of the interest rate, the auction outcome is called "all hold," and the interest rate is reset at an "all-hold rate," usually a low rate specified in the bond prospectus.

[10]Maximum auction rates may be rather high, especially for MARS. For example, some MARS issued by the Port Authority of New York were reset to 20 percent after their auctions failed in mid-February 2008. Maximum rates for SLARS are often designed to keep the issuer's interest payments low to ensure a high credit rating (Austin, 2008). For example, some bonds cap their total interest payments within the past 90 days, resulting in very low maximum rates, sometimes even zero, after their auctions have failed a few times.

[11]ARS guidelines by major dealers generally follow closely the recommendations by the Securities Industry and Financial Markets Association (SIFMA). Specifically, section 4.3.5 of SIFMA (2007) suggests that "a Broker-Dealer should disclose to Existing Owners and other Bidders" that "(b) it routinely places one or more Bids in Auctions generally to prevent a Failed Auction or a Clearing Rate the Broker-Dealer believes is not a market Rate at the time it makes its Bid, even after obtaining knowledge of some or all of the other Orders, but is not obligated to continue to place such Bids or to bid in any particular Auction."

2.4 The Collapse of the ARS Market

The subprime mortgage crisis in the summer of 2007 caused an overall revaluation of complex structured securities and credit risks. Investors started to raise concerns about the credit quality of some ARS, especially those insured or issued by major troubled bond insurers such as Ambac Financial Group, Inc., MBIA Inc., and Financial Guaranty Insurance Company (FGIC). In late 2007, auction failures started to occur for some ARPS, including those issued by troubled bond insurers.[12]

Moreover, exposures to the credit crisis put significant strains on auction dealers' overall balance sheets. Liquidity provision and market making became increasingly expensive across all over-the-counter markets (Froot, 2009). On January 22, 2008, the first day that bond investors could react to Fitch Ratings's downgrade of Ambac, Lehman Brothers Holdings decided not to bid on two auctions it ran, resulting in the first MARS auction failure since 1991.[13] While Lehman's action did not spill over to other auction dealers, perhaps because of its selective nature, it did intensify concerns about possible withdrawals of liquidity supports by other dealers.[14] On February 12, news broke that Goldman Sachs had withdrawn liquidity supports on all auctions it ran and that Citigroup had also let fail a selected set of its auctions.[15] On the following days, other major investment banks, including Citigroup, Lehman Brothers, Merrill Lynch, and UBS, all reportedly stopped supporting their auctions.[16] As word of dealers' withdrawal and auction failures spread through major news outlets, auctions began to fail en masse. For example, on February 13, the auction failure rate reportedly peaked to about 85 percent (Austin, 2008). Since then, failure rates have declined somewhat but have remained frequently above 60 percent. Responding to the ARS market failures, the Securities Exchange Commission (SEC) on March 14, 2008, allowed municipal bond issuers to bid in their own auctions.

The collapse of the ARS market led to serious consequences. ARS investors, including big corporations, such as Bristol-Meyers Squibb, Jet Blue, and Palm, Inc., and many high-net-

---

[12]See, for example, Bloomberg news, "Rigged Bids, SEC Help Dealers as Auction Bonds Fail," reported by Michael Quint, November 21, 2007.

[13]The only previous failed MARS auction happened in June 1990 to an industrial development bond issued by Tucson Electric Power Co., Pima County. The bond, insured by Financial Securities Assurance and rated AAA at issuance, was issued in 1988 as the first MARS ever. Goldman Sachs was the bond's original underwriter. In 1991, after 16 consecutive failures, the bond's new auction dealer, The Bear Stearns Companies, Inc., converted it to a fixed-rate bond (*The Bond Buyer*, October 3, 1991).

[14]See, for example, Bloomberg news, "Nevada Power Auction-Rate Woes Test Banks' Support of Debt," reported by Martin Z. Braun, January 30, 2008.

[15]See, for example, Bloomberg news, "Municipal Market Is Beset by Wave of Auction-Bond Failures," reported by Martin Z. Braun, February 12, 2008.

[16]See, for example, Bloomberg news, " "Merrill Reduces Support for Auction-Rate Securities, People Say," reported by Beth Williams and Michael Weiss, February 14, 2008

worth retirees, suddenly found their "cash equivalent" investments inaccessible (Comment, 2010). Some ARS issuers struggled to pay interest rates as high as 20 percent. Auction dealers were entangled in costly lawsuits claiming they misrepresented the product as safe and liquid. Although these issues have captured headlines in the media, our concerns in this paper are deeper. We are interested both in the determinants of auction clearing prices when the market functioned and in the economic forces behind the collapse of the market—in particular, the fragility of discretionary liquidity provision during systemic events.

3 Data and Sampling

Our overall sample consists of all MARS whose auctions are run by three major auction agents and whose transactions are subjected to the reporting requirements by the Municipal Securities Rulemaking Board (MSRB). In this section, we describe the data on auction results, intraday transactions, and bond characteristics, and we discuss the sampling and summary statistics.

3.1 Data on Auction Results

We obtained proprietary reports of daily auction results from three major auction agents: Deutsche Bank, Wilmington Trust, and Bank of New York Mellon.[17] The reports we received from Deutsche Bank start on January 1, 2007, and those from Wilmington Trust and Bank of New York Mellon start on July 1, 2007. All reports end on April 21, 2008.

The auction reports contain the following information on each auction: auction date, bond CUSIP number, auction dealer or lead manager, auction frequency, auction status (failed, succeeded, or all hold), reset interest rate, benchmark rate (for example, 30-day Libor or 7-day commercial paper rate), and bond insurer. Benchmark rates are the index rates used in calculating the maximum auction rates.

The auction reports cover all types of ARS. But we focus on the bonds that have also appeared in the MSRB intraday transactions data. These bonds consist of MARS issued by state and local governments, as well as a small portion of SLARS issued by student loan authorities. Since these SLARS also fall into the MSRB's reporting requirements, we treat them as municipal bonds.

---

[17]Four major auction agents operate in the ARS market. The fourth agent is Wells Fargo, which mainly handles ARPS and SLARS. Auction agents differ from auction dealers in that auction agents simply provide bookkeeping services and the technical platform for auctions. Unlike auction dealers, auction agents do not interact with investors and do not affect auction results.

3.2 Intraday Transaction Data

Municipal securities dealers are required by the MSRB to report, almost in real time, each purchase and sale transaction. Transactions of MARS, either conducted through auctions or intermediated by dealers outside auctions, are subjected to the same reporting requirements.[18]

For all trades, the MSRB transactions data contain information on price, date and time of the trade, par value traded, and whether the trade is a dealer buy from a customer, a dealer sell to a customer, or a trade between dealers. Each bond is identified by its CUSIP number, which allows us to merge the data with the bond description data discussed later. The MSRB transactions data play an important role in our analysis because we use them to estimate dealers' backstop bids in auctions and how they manage their inventories dynamically.

3.3 Data on Bond Characteristics

Both the auction reports and the transactions data have only limited information on bond characteristics. We obtained from Bloomberg additional bond description data, including bond type (general obligation (GO) or revenue), tax status (tax-exempt or taxable), credit enhancement (insurance), underlying credit rating (issue's rating in the absence of credit enhancement), dates of issuance and maturity, and par amount outstanding. However, the information on one key variable, the maximum auction rate, is only partially available: maximum auction rates are the same as reset rates for failed auction, but are not readily available for successful auctions in any data sources.

Maximum auction rates are determined according to the rules specified in debt contracts. Broadly speaking, the rules are either fixed or floating (multiplicative, additive, or complex). We classify these rules as follows: fixed—for example, 15 percent; multiplicative, a multiple of the chosen benchmark rate; additive, the benchmark rate plus a fixed markup; or complex, usually a combination of the aforementioned types, possibly linked to interest paid in the past.[19] Often, these multiples or markups vary with credit ratings.

Instead of reading through all bond prospectuses, we first used a statistical method to infer the rules for calculating maximum rates. First, because maximum rates are linear functions of benchmark rates in fixed, multiplicative, and additive rules, we could infer the

---

[18]Specifically, the MSRB's Rule G-14 states that "a dealer effecting trades in short-term instruments under nine months in effective maturity, including variable rate instruments, auction rate products, and commercial paper, shall report such trades by the end of the Business Day on which the trades were executed." See "Rule G-14 RTRS Procedures," item (a)(ii)(B), www.msrb.org/msrb1/rules/rulesg14.html.

[19]This "look back" feature is commonly seen in SLARS. For example, a bond may have multiplicative maximum auction rate as long as the 90-day rolling average interest rate does not surpass a threshold that is based on an average Treasury rate over the same period.

rule accurately by using data from at least two failed auctions. Second, for bonds that had failed only once over the entire period, we inferred the rule based on the following criteria: The rule is fixed if the auction rate is a multiple of 1 percent; otherwise, the rule is multiplicative if the ratio of the maximum rate to the benchmark rate, rounded to 1 percent, is a multiple of 25 percent; and the rule is additive if the difference between the maximum rate and the benchmark rate, rounded to 1/1000 of 1 percent, is a multiple of one-half of 1 percent.

The potential issues with our statistical method are the following: (i) It does not work if the rule is complex or if the bond had never failed; (ii) for bonds with only one failed auction, we identify the rules with some tolerance of error; and (iii) errors may also occur if the issuers changed the rules after auction failures, which does happen but only rarely.

Leaving out bonds in (i) may potentially introduce selection bias into our analysis. To address the selection issue, we manually collected information on bonds whose maximum-rate rules we could not identify by using the statistical method just discussed. To check the estimation errors in (ii) and (iii), we looked up the prospectuses of a random sample of bonds whose maximum-rate rules we determined using our statistical method. For these bonds, we found fairly low estimation errors.

3.4 Sampling and Summary Statistics

Table 1 shows how our sample is constructed. There are 4,945 ARS in all reports from the three auction agents (line 1), of which 3,709 are municipal securities, as they appear at least once in the MSRB's transactions report (line 2). For 3,567 of these municipal securities, information on their bond characteristics is available through Bloomberg (line 3). For our analysis, we removed bonds with reset periods shorter than 7 days or longer than 35 days. This adjustment left us with 3,526 bonds, which we labeled as our "overall sample" (line 4). As shown on line 5, for 2,845 bonds in the overall sample, we were able to identify the types of their maximum-rate rules and compute their maximum rates using either a statistical or a manual identification method.

Table 2 shows the summary statistics. Our overall sample consists of 2,463 bonds issued by non-student-loan municipalities with total par outstanding of $137 billion (83 percent of the entire non-student-loan MARS market) and 1,063 bonds issued by student loan authorities with total par outstanding of $52 billion (61 percent of the entire SLARS market).[20]

In our overall sample, only about 1.5 percent of the bonds are GO bonds, and 17 percent

---

[20]According to estimates from Merrill Lynch, at the end of 2007, total par outstanding of bonds issued by non-student-loan municipal issuers was $166 billion, and total SLARS outstanding, issued by either municipal authorities or private companies, was $86 billion.

are taxable. Most of the bonds have reset periods of 7, 28, or 35 days (45, 18, or 37 percent, respectively). Roughly 41 percent of the bonds have no underlying rating. Among those that do, more than one-half have an underlying rating of A or better. Forty-one percent of all bonds are insured by "weak insurers"—those under review for downgrades during the sample period, including Ambac, MBIA, FGIC, CFIG Guaranty, and XL Capital Insurance (XLCA), 11 percent are insured by "strong insurers," including Financial Security Assurance (FSA) and Assured Guaranty, and the rest are either insured by other small insurers (20 percent) or not insured (28 percent). Two of the three auction agents provide the identities of auction dealers directly in their daily reports. When auction dealers were not reported, we used the "lead manager" as reported in Bloomberg to identify the auction dealer. Our inventory calculation is based on this selected dealer. As an auction dealer, Citigroup, UBS, and Morgan Stanley together account for about one-half of the bonds (22, 18, and 10 percent, respectively), and the top five broker-dealers account for nearly two-thirds of the bonds. On average, the bonds have $54 million of par outstanding, a minimum bidding size of $40,000, and 24 years to maturity. In general, the foregoing summary statistics change only slightly when we restrict our sample to bonds with known maximum rates.

Table 3 shows descriptive statistics on maximum auction rates.[21] As shown in panel A, among the 2,845 bonds with known maximum-rate rules, 1,143, or 40 percent, have fixed maximum rates. Most of the bonds with floating rules (1,404 of 1,702, or more than 80 percent) have multiplicative rules. We can also see that MARS with fixed maximum rates are less likely to have failed auctions. About three-fourths of bonds with a fixed cap never experienced auction failures during the sample period, while more than 90 percent of bonds with a floating cap had at least one failed auction.

MARS with fixed maximum rates tend to have higher maximum auction rates. As shown in panel B, the average maximum rate on bonds with fixed rules is about 14 percent, significantly higher than that on bonds with floating rules—under 7 percent. The distributions of maximum rates also differ significantly by their calculation rules. As shown in figure 3, while the maximum rates of bonds with floating rules distribute fairly continuously in their ranges, those bonds with fixed rules mostly concentrate on 12 percent and 15 percent.

We broke the sample into three periods: the pre-crisis period from July 1, 2007, to December 31, 2007; the crisis period from February 11, 2008, to February 19, 2008; and the post-crisis period from February 27, 2008, to March 19, 2008. Our results are robust to some alternative choices of cutoff points.[22]

---

[21]We can identify the maximum-rate rules for 90 percent of the bonds that had never failed or failed only once during our sampling period (982 of 1,094 and 332 of 364, respectively) and for 75 percent of bonds that had two or more failed auctions (1,542 of 2,068).

[22]Results are qualitatively similar if we use July 1, 2007, to January 21, 2008, as the pre-crisis period;

4 Empirical Analysis

In this section, we first provide quantitative evidence that auction dealers effectively acted as market makers in the ARS auctions until the collapse of the ARS market. We then show that this marketmaking role significantly affected net investor demand and auction clearing rates. Finally, we present evidence that auction dealers' implicit commitment to making markets is fragile. In particular, we argue that, consistent with the theory of implicit contracts, auction dealers forfeited reputational capital in favor of preserving financial capital when their survival was under threat. Moreover, such fragility was exacerbated by reputational externality among major auction dealers.

4.1 Evidence on the Role of Auction Dealers

To seek quantitative evidence on the role of auction dealers in the ARS market, we used the MSRB transactions data to estimate the extent to which dealers bid on their own accounts in the auctions, the way they managed their inventories, and their actions through the collapse of the ARS market.

4.1.1 Estimating Auction Trades Using Transactions Data

As mentioned in section 2, auction dealers generally disclose in their ARS guidelines or bond prospectuses that they may routinely bid in the auctions. However, no disclosure is made on the actual occurrence or the purposes of such bids. In addition, the auction reports we obtained from auction agents contained no information on the actual bids in the auctions. We used the MSRB transactions data to address this data issue.

Our estimation assumed that all trades on auction dates were from orders filled in auctions regardless of the auction's running time. We called these trades "auction trades." Conversely, we called all trades executed in between auction dates "non-auction trades." Such an assumption was necessary because the MSRB transactions data have no indicator for whether a trade is executed in or outside an auction. In addition, while the transactions data do have a time stamp for each trade, we lacked comprehensive data on the running time of each auction.[23]

February 20, 2008, to March 19, 2009, as the post-crisis period; and the period in between as the crisis period. We considered these alternative cutoff points because January 22, 2008, marked the first MARS auction failure, February 12 marked the first overall withdrawal of liquidity support by major auction dealers, and March 20 marked the start of issuers' participation in bidding after the SEC's rule change. In addition, starting from late March, many issuers ramped up their efforts to refinance or convert their ARS to either fixed-rate bonds or variable-rate demand notes.

[23]In theory, this assumption may result in underestimating the amount of non-auction trades because trades that happened on auction dates, but prior to auction opening or after auction closing, are actually

Sell orders by existing bondholders and bid orders by new bondholders filled in auctions are reported as "dealer buys from customers" and "dealer sells to customers," respectively. The difference between dealer buys and dealer sells on auction dates, or "net dealer buys," is our estimate of the amount of bids submitted by auction dealers on their own accounts. For ease of exposition, we also labeled total dealer buys from customers "gross dealer buys," which measure gross liquidity demand from investors in each auction.

4.1.2 Auction Dealers as Market Makers

We first present evidence that auction dealers provided a significant amount of liquidity support in the pre-crisis auctions. Figure 4 shows the average par amount of gross and net dealer buys per auction from July 1, 2007, to March 19, 2008. Over the second half of 2007, when the ARS market was largely stable, the average gross dealer buys per auction fluctuated around the average of $4.2 million (with a standard deviation of $0.75 million), while the average net dealer buys was about $1.8 million. In other words, on a typical auction day during normal times, auction dealers would purchase on their own accounts over 40 percent of the dollar amount of ARS sold by investors.

More strikingly, auction dealers were the sole bidders in a large fraction of the auctions. In figure 5, we plot the distribution of the ratio of net dealer buys to gross dealer buys for successful auctions (excluding all-hold auctions) during the second half of 2007. As we can see, for nearly one-fourth of the auctions, the ratio of net-to-gross dealer buys equals 1. That is, for these auctions, there were no investor bids at all, and auction dealers were the only bidders to buy the entire supply of sell orders.

Now, how did auction dealers manage the inventories that they obtained from providing liquidity in the auctions? In figure 6, we contrast average par amount of net dealer buys on auction dates with that in between the current and the next auctions. During the pre-crisis period, dealers had been net buyers in auctions and net sellers after auctions. That is, like market makers, they absorbed surplus supply of ARS in auctions into their inventories and then unloaded them after auctions in the non-auction secondary market. Unlike the trades of market makers in other over-the-counter markets, all pre-crisis trades in and out of auctions happened mostly at par. So auction dealers were not directly compensated through markups. They were, however, paid on a fixed-fee basis to be the managers of the auctions.[24]

---

non-auction trades. However, from our examinations of a randomly selected sample of auctions, almost all trades reported on auction dates were executed during the running times of the auctions. A small number of trades happened after the auctions ended, and they were generally dealer sells to customers. Thus, the measurement error from counting all trades on auction dates as auction trades is small and, if anything, biases against our finding of dealers supporting auctions.

[24]The fees are paid irrespective of the outcome of the auction. Issuers whose auctions have failed since

4.1.3   Major Dealers Stopped Making Markets

Figure 6 also shows that the dynamics of the ARS market changed significantly in late 2007 and early 2008. Auction dealers were taking increasingly larger amounts of bonds in auctions.[25] Meanwhile, dealers continued to unload their inventories, though at a noticeably slower pace, in the non-auction secondary market. The average net dealer sells (negative net dealer buys) in the non-auction secondary market stayed in their usual range until the end of February, when dealers experienced major difficulties in offloading bonds in the non-auction market.

The sharp drop in net dealer buys on February 13 was due to the decisions of major dealers to stop supporting auctions. To present a clearer picture of the market dynamics during the week of February 12, 2008, we plot in figure 7 the fraction of auctions that failed to clear for each of the top 10 auction dealers (ranked by market share). On February 12, Goldman Sachs became the first dealer that allowed all its auctions with insufficient bids to fail. Citigroup also *selectively* let some of its auctions fail on the same day.[26] Over the next three days, other major dealers followed suit.

In the next two subsections, we analyze the effect of auction dealers' marketmaking on net investor demand and auction clearing rates by contrasting the market dynamics with and without dealers' liquidity support.

4.2   Investor Demand Shortfall

4.2.1   Definition

We estimated net investor demand by the incidence of investor demand shortfall (IDS)— a situation in which investor bid orders are not sufficient to cover all investor sell orders. Because we had no auction bidding information, we did not observe directly the dollar amount of net investor demand.[27] However, we could infer the incidence of IDS from auction outcome and transactions data.

Our estimation method was based on the following observation (also discussed in sec-

---

the crisis have continued to pay auction dealers the management fees.

[25]On December 15, 2007, David Shulman (UBS municipal finance director) stated the following in an e-mail to Joseph Scoby (UBS chief risk officer): "(I) will need some guidance ... in terms of our overall position and philosophy as it relates to continuing to support these auctions ... What is clear is that the fundamental mechanism of the ARCs (ARS) structure is not working in a liquidity squeezed environment ... " (Commonwealth of Massachusetts (2008), p. 6).

[26]See, for example, Bloomberg News, "Municipal Market Is Beset by Wave of Auction-Bond Failures," reported by Martin Z. Braun, February 12, 2008. Also, see Bergstresser, Cole and Shenai, 2009.

[27]It is impossible to estimate the dollar amount of IDS because unfilled bid orders in successful auctions and unfilled sell orders in failed auctions are not observable.

tion 2). When an IDS occurs, the outcome of an auction has only two possibilities. The first is "pseudo failure," in which the auction dealer provides support bids on its own account and the auction appears successful. In the data, this outcome corresponds to the case when the net dealer buy is positive on auction day. The second possible auction outcome is "actual failure," in which the auction dealer does not provide supporting bids and lets the auction fail. Therefore, the occurrence of IDS is observationally equivalent to either actual failure or pseudo failure.

Before discussing the econometric model on the determinants of IDS, we present a few time-series properties of the average incidence of IDS. In figure 8, we plot the rate of IDS and its two components over our study period. Before January 22, 2008, IDS consists almost solely of pseudo failures, because auction dealers routinely supported the auctions. The IDS rate was largely stationary, averaging about 55 percent with a range between 40 and 70 percent.[28] The rate crept up steadily after Lehman Brothers let two of its MARS auctions fail on January 22. Investors became increasingly concerned about the possible withdrawal of liquidity supports by auction dealers. Then Goldman Sachs withdrew its support to all of its MARS auctions on February 12, and other major auction dealers followed suit the next day. As a result, pseudo-failure rates fell sharply, but the actual failure rate jumped to nearly 60 percent. The IDS rate peaked at 90 percent on February 13, stayed at around 80 percent until February 27, and then trended down to about 65 percent and consisted of mostly actual failures in the rest of the sample period.

The time series of IDS suggests that the ARS market roughly went through three phases: from a pre-crisis equilibrium, through a transition period during which auction dealers stopped making markets, to a post-crisis equilibrium. The constant need for liquidity support from auction dealers in the pre-crisis auctions highlights a lack of depth in these auctions. The extent of this inherent demand imbalance was not observable by investors before the crisis due to the lack of disclosure. After auction dealers stopped making markets, the demand imbalance became observable through auction failures.

4.2.2 Modelling Equilibrium Investor Demand Shortfall

We used a probit regression approach to analyze the determinants of IDS in the pre- and post-crisis equilibriums. We specified our empirical models under the guidance of existing auction theories. Specifically, for the post-crisis period, without auction dealers acting as the bidder of last resort, ARS auctions closely resemble standard uniform-price auctions.

---

[28]Our result is consistent with anecdotal evidence in the complaint against UBS filed by the state of Massachusetts. Among the MARS and SLARS auctions run by UBS from January 1, 2006 and February 28, 2008, about 86 percent would have failed if UBS had not submitted support bids (Commonwealth of Massachusetts (2008), p. 40).

Existing theories on such auctions suggest that, all else being equal, the likelihood of IDS decreases with the maximum auction rate and increases with the fundamental value of the bond yield (see Proposition 1 of Back and Zender, 1993).[29]

For the pre-crisis period, with auction dealers acting as the bidders of last resort, ARS auctions resemble uniform-price auctions with endogenous supply. Auction theories suggest that such auctions are more competitive and that auction clearing rates approach bond fundamental values as the number of bidders increases (Back and Zender, 2001; Wang and Zender, 2002; Damianov, 2005; LiCalzi and Pavan, 2005; McAdams, 2007). However, theories provide us with little guidance in predicting when an IDS may occur in these auctions. The literature focuses squarely on the equilibriums in which sellers never need to adjust their supply ex post and insufficient bidding never occurs. However, we argue that if dealers always intervene in auctions, then investors expect auctions to never fail and auction outcomes to be competitive. Thus, investors' demand for liquidity will not be related to either the maximum auction rate or the bond fundamental value.

We summarize these hypotheses as follows:

Hypothesis 1 (1) In the pre-crisis period, when auction dealers act as the bidders of last resort, the likelihood of IDS is unrelated to either maximum auction rates or bond fundamental values; (2) In the post-crisis period, when auction dealers stop making markets, the likelihood of IDS is positively related to the fundamental value of the bond yield but negatively related to the maximum auction rate.

Thus, for both the pre- and post-crisis equilibriums, we considered the maximum auction rate and the following variables that approximate the bond's fundamental value as the potential determinants of IDS: (1) bond characteristics, including bond size (in log), age (time since issuance, in log), remaining maturity (in log), and whether the bond is backed by student loans, is a GO bond, is issued for refunding purposes, or is taxable; (2) credit risk factors, including indicators for underlying bond ratings and for credit enhancements (specifically, we indicate whether the bond is insured by strong insurers, including FSA and Assured Guaranty which retained their AAA ratings, or by weak insurers, including Ambac, MBIA, FGIC, CFIG, and XLCA, which were under review for downgrades and in the headline news in early 2008); (3) other auction design factors, such as interest rate reset frequency, and minimum bid size—variables that may affect the liquidity of the bond; and (4) general municipal bond market conditions, including the one-year municipal bond yield, municipal bond term spread, and volatility of the swap rate.

---

[29] The extensive auction literature almost always focuses on the equilibriums when auctions clear. To the best of our knowledge, Back and Zender (1993) is the only study that contains explicit analysis on the possibility of undersubscription in uniform-price auctions.

We also took into account some features that are unique to ARS auctions as compared with standard uniform-price auctions. In particular, liquidity conditions in the non-auction secondary market may affect bidding strategies and valuations in the auctions. We used the average number of non-auction secondary-market trades during the interauction period just prior to each auction to measure liquidity in the non-auction secondary market.

To summarize, the latent decision variable Y_{it} for our probit regression of IDS is a linear function $f(x)$ of the following variables:

$$\begin{aligned} Y_{it} = f(&\text{bonds: size, remaining mat., age, taxable, student loan, GO, refunding;} \\ &\text{auction: maximum auction rate, reset period, minimum bid size;} \\ &\text{credit risk: underlying rating, insurer strength;} \\ &\text{municipal bond markets: munis term spread, volatility of swap rate;} \\ &\text{non-auction liquidity: non-auction trading freq.}). \end{aligned} \tag{1}$$

4.2.3 Determinants of Investor Demand Shortfall

Pooled Regressions for the Pre- and Post-Crisis Periods

We first estimated our probit models with pooled samples for the pre- and post-crisis periods. The results for the pre-crisis period, from July 1, 2007, to December 31, 2007, are reported in columns 1-4 in table 4, while those for the post-crisis period, from February 27, 2008, to March 19, 2008, are in columns 5-8.[30]

Two findings are striking. First, our models can explain a significant fraction of the variation in IDS in the post-crisis period but only a small fraction of the variation in the pre-crisis period. In the post-crisis period, the pseudo R^2 of the full specification (column 7) reaches nearly 45 percent. Consistent with auction theories, without auction dealers making markets, net investor demand is strongly related to fundamental risk factors and auction design variables. In contrast, the pseudo-R^2s are only 2 percent in the regressions for the pre-crisis period. This result suggests that with auction dealers making the market, the occurrence of insufficient investor bids was driven largely by ARS investors' idiosyncratic liquidity shocks that were not correlated with bond fundamental values and auction characteristics. This finding also supports our hypothesis that investors did not consider auction failures a significant risk in the pre-crisis period.

---

[30]We have experimented with alternative starting points for the post-crisis sample, ranging from February 18 to March 3. The general results are largely the same as reported here. The sample ends on March 19 because, after that, issuers started to aggressively refinance or convert their ARS to fixed-rate bonds or variable-rate demand notes. In addition, the SEC issued a directive on March 14 to allow issuers to bid in the auctions of their own ARS. These activities led to substantial changes in the market structures.

Second, the maximum auction rate was the most important determinant of IDS after auction dealers stopped making markets. In the post-crisis regressions, the pseudo R^2s increase from 19 percent in column (6) to nearly 45 percent in column (7) once the maximum rate is added to the model. The likelihood of IDS is strongly and negatively related to the maximum rate. All else being equal, the likelihood of IDS decreases 17 percentage points if the maximum rate increases 1 standard deviation (4 percentage points). In contrast, in the pre-crisis regressions, the pseudo R^2s change little whether or not the maximum auction rate is included as an independent variable. The marginal effect of the maximum rate (columns 3 and 4) is significant statistically but is small in magnitude.

To highlight the change in the importance of the maximum auction rate to explaining IDS, we plot in figure 9 the time series of the rate of IDS by maximum rate. Here, a maximum auction rate is classified as high if it is greater than 10 percent, and low otherwise. The cutoff point, 10 percent, is about the median maximum rate in our sample. Overall, before auction dealers withdrew their liquidity support in the week of February 12, 2008, the rate of IDS among bonds with high maximum rates was indistinguishable from the rate among those with low maximum rates. After that, the market quickly bifurcated. For bonds with low maximum rates, the rate of IDS shot up and stayed close to 100 percent, while for bonds with high maximum rates, the rate of IDS trended down to about 40 percent.

Other interesting results are as follows. In the pre-crisis period, the likelihood of IDS is positively related to bond size, student loan backing, and tax-exemption status (see the full specification in table 4 column 3). In particular, the likelihoods of IDS for tax-exempt bonds and SLARS are, respectively, about 11 and 8 percentage points higher than for other comparable bonds. The likelihood of IDS is only weakly and negatively related to a better underlying rating but strongly and positively related to the slope of the municipal bond yield curve.

In the post-crisis period, the likelihood of IDS is also positively related to bond size, but to a lesser extent. The likelihood of IDS is also higher for older bonds. Interestingly, SLARS become 17 percentage points more likely than other comparable bonds to experience IDS. In contrast to the pre-crisis period, the likelihood of IDS for taxable bonds is 7 percentage points higher than for comparable tax-exempt bonds. In addition, bonds that were insured by weak insurers are more likely to experience IDS, reflecting the deepened concerns over the financial strength of troubled monoline insurers. Also, the underlying rating becomes significant: Bonds with underlying ratings equal to or better than AA are 7 percentage points less likely to experience IDS than other comparable bonds. This finding suggests that as the value of credit enhancements depreciated during the crisis, investors paid more attention to the issuer's underlying creditworthiness. Finally, the likelihood of IDS becomes significantly and positively associated with a longer reset frequency but unrelated to the term structure of the municipal bond yield curve.

Weekly Regressions

The regressions suggest that the determinants of net investor demand changed substantially after auction dealers withdrew their liquidity support. To obtain a dynamic view of this change, we ran probit regressions of IDS on weekly samples using the specification in equation (1). In figure 10, we plot the weekly time series of two key statistics, the pseudo R^2 and the coefficient of the maximum auction rate, obtained from these regressions. As shown in the top panel, the pseudo R^2 stayed below 5 percent for the entire second half of 2007. It started to tick up in early 2008 but remained below 10 percent until the week of February 12, 2008, when auction dealers withdrew their liquidity support. It then shot up to more than 40 percent. As shown in the lower panel, before the week of February 12, the coefficient of the maximum rate stayed just above zero, and for about half the time, it was not statistically significant from zero. When auction dealers withdrew their liquidity support, the coefficient fell sharply to significantly below zero.

The dynamics of the pseudo R^2s and the coefficients of the maximum rate confirm what we found in the pooled regressions. That is, when auction dealers acted as the bidders of last resort, net investor demand was driven largely by investors' idiosyncratic liquidity shocks. But after auction dealers withdrew their support, net investor demand depended importantly on the maximum auction rate and bond fundamental values.

4.2.4   IDS during Transition: Information Based or Panic Driven

We now study IDS during the transition period. The surge in the rate of IDS during the week of February 12, 2008, may have been caused by two factors: either new information on bond fundamentals or a self-fulfilling panic (Cass and Shell, 1983; Diamond and Dybvig, 1983; Gorton, 1985; Jacklin and Bhattacharya, 1988). In our case, rising IDS may be information driven if key risk factors that affect ARS valuations change sharply. These key risk factors include the expected likelihood that auction dealers will withdraw their liquidity supports, as well as the credit risk on the bonds. The odds that dealers will abandon the market are bounded by certainty, as realized in the post-crisis period. Thus, the probability of IDS predicted by the model estimated using the *post-crisis sample* would be the upper bound of the IDS rate if IDS were completely information-based. Therefore, the difference between the observed IDS rate and the predicted upper bound, which we call the "abnormal IDS rate," is our conservative gauge of panic-driven IDS.

Specifically, we first computed the predicted probability of IDS during the transition period using the probit model estimated from the post-crisis sample (table 4, column 7). Then the abnormal IDS rate equals the observed IDS rate minus the average predicted probability of IDS.

Our approach for estimating the abnormal IDS rate resembles that used in the standard event studies (see, for example, Campbell, Lo and MacKinlay, 1997). The notable difference is that our estimation window, the post-crisis period, is after the event window (the week of February 12) instead of prior to the event window. This "reverse" event-study approach has also been used in Calomiris and Mason (2003) in their study of the effect of contagion on bank failures.

As shown in table 5, the abnormal IDS rates are statistically significant and positive during the entire transition period. The abnormal failure rates average about 13 percent over the period and peak on February 13 at 21 percent, or about 23 percent of the observed IDS rate. Again, this estimate for the portion of the IDS rates that cannot be explained by information-based factors is conservative. Thus, we conclude that a significant portion of IDS in the week of February 12 was due to a self-fulfilling panic.

4.3 Auction Clearing Rates

We now examine how auction clearing rates changed when auction dealers withdrew their liquidity supports. We find that in the pre-crisis period, auction clearing rates were strongly associated with proxies for fundamental values but only weakly associated with auction design. In contrast, in the post-crisis period, auction clearing rates were only weakly associated with proxies for fundamental values but strongly associated with auction design, particularly the maximum auction rate. These results are consistent with the predictions of existing auction theories.

4.3.1 The Average ARS Clearing Rates

We first examined the average ARS clearing rates during our sample period. In figure 11, we plot the ratios of average auction clearing rates in our sample to one-month Libor. We used the ratios to control for the general conditions in the short-term credit market. To compare the dynamics of the ARS market with those of other short-term municipal bond markets, we also plot the ratios of two other short-term municipal bond rates, the SIFMA seven-day swap index and the one-year municipal bond index from Municipal Market Adviser (MMA), to one-month Libor. The SIFMA seven-day swap index is an average rate of a selected sample of variable-rate demand notes (VRDNs). Like ARS, VRDNs are long-term municipal bonds with their rates reset periodically. However, VRDNs differ importantly from ARS in that VRDNs have an explicit put option that allows investors to sell the bonds back at par to the remarketing agent. In contrast to the implicit liquidity support for ARS auctions, the put option embedded in VRDNs is contractually guaranteed by a liquidity provider.[31] The MMA one-year municipal bond index is a survey-based bond yield index, reflecting the market's assessments of the one-year yield for a representative municipal bond issuer.

As we can see, the ARS clearing rates closely followed other comparable short-term rates in the pre-crisis period but became substantially higher than other rates after the crisis. Until early December, the ARS clearing rates, like the SIFMA swap rates and the MMA one-year rates, all stayed at about 70 percent of one-month Libor. Since then, the ARS clearing rates diverged from the other two series, climbing more than 100 percent of Libor in late January. The divergence widened sharply on February 13, when major auction dealers withdrew their liquidity support to the auctions. The fact that other short-term municipal bond rates did not rise during the crisis suggests that what happened in the ARS market was not the result of the changes in either the fundamental credit risk of municipal bond issuers or the associated risk premium. This finding is contrary to the claim by McConnell and Saretto (2010) that auction failures were due to a sharp deterioration in ARS fundamental values.

4.3.2 The Determinants of ARS Clearing Rates

We used a regression approach to examine how the determinants of auction clearing rates changed after auction dealers withdrew their liquidity support. The independent variables are the same as those described in equation (1). To guide our empirical analysis and interpretation, we first used existing auction theories to develop testable hypotheses on auction clearing rates.

We hypothesized that in the pre-crisis period, reset rates were strongly related to bonds' fundamental values but weakly related to auction designs. As is commonly done in auction theories, we referred to fundamental value as the interest rate that a bond would earn in a competition equilibrium. As discussed earlier, ARS auctions with dealers placing supporting bids resemble uniform-price auctions with sellers being able to adjust the supply *after* observing all bids. Existing theories suggest that these endogenous-supply auctions are competitive and that the auction clearing rates would approach fundamental values when the number of bidders increases (see, for example, Back and Zender, 2001).

In contrast, we hypothesized that in the post-crisis period, auction reset rates may deviate

---

[31]Another notable difference between VRDNs and ARS is that VRDNs' reset rates are determined by remarketing agents instead of auctions.

from fundamental values and be *positively* related to maximum auction rates. The reason is that theories on uniform-price auctions without liquidity support suggest that there may exist a continuum of equilibriums. The equilibrium with the highest clearing rate—the maximum interest rate—is always most preferable to bidders. Such an equilibrium is achievable when bidders tacitly collude (see, for example, Wilson, 1979, Back and Zender, 1993).

In sum, we hypothesized the following:

Hypothesis 2 (1) In the pre-crisis period, when broker-dealers acted as the bidders of last resort, auction reset rates were strongly related to the proxies for bond fundamental values but not to auction design characteristics, such as the maximum auction rate; (2) In the post-crisis period, auction reset rates were weakly related to the proxies for bond fundamental values but positively and significantly related to the maximum auction rate.

4.3.3 Regression Results

We report the ordinary least squares regression results in table 6. All regressions are restricted to the sample of successful auctions. We cluster all standard errors at the issuer level.

Consistent with our hypotheses, we find that reset rates are strongly related to the fundamental values of the bonds in the pre-crisis auctions. As shown in the left panel, the R^2 in the specification with only fundamental variables (column (1)) is 63 percent. Variables that have statistically significant coefficients have signs consistent with conventional views on bond valuations. Specifically, taxable bonds have higher reset rates than tax-exempt bonds; bonds backed by student loans have higher rates than those backed by states' taxing powers (GO bonds); bonds that are wrapped by both strong and weak insurers have lower rates than unwrapped bonds, as monoline insurers all appeared healthy before the current financial crisis; bonds with underlying ratings equal to or better than AA also have lower rates, by about 13 basis points, than unrated bonds; and reset rates are positively related to both municipal bond term spread and interest rate volatility.

Also as we hypothesized, auction design characteristics matter only marginally for reset rates in the pre-crisis period. The regression with auction variables, such as maximum auction rates, as additional controls has only a slightly higher R^2. The coefficient on the maximum rate, albeit statistically significant, is quantitatively small. Based on the full model (column (2)), for a 1 percentage point increase in the maximum rate, reset rates are just over 1 basis point higher.

In contrast, results for the post-crisis auctions, shown in the right panel, indicate that reset rates were weakly related to the fundamental values of the bonds after auction dealers stopped supporting the auctions. The R^2 in the specification with only the proxies for bond fundamentals (column (3)) is only 27 percent. The signs of some coefficients on bond fundamentals deviate from the conventional view of bond valuation. In particular, reset rates on insured bonds, even those with strong insurers, are significantly higher, both statistically and economically, than such rates on uninsured bonds. This result suggests that investors indiscriminately shied away from all insured bonds at a time when investors were concerned about the financial strength of monoline insurers. Also, the coefficients on student loan indicators are not statistically significant anymore, and the coefficients on the municipal bond term spread are negative and statistically insignificant.

Most notably, the reset rates are significantly and positively related to maximum auction rates. The coefficient on the maximum rate is much larger in magnitude compared with the pre-crisis period. Based on the full model (column (4)), for a 1 percentage point increase in the maximum rate, reset rates are 14 basis points higher. To highlight the change in the importance of the maximum rate, figure 12 plots the average ARS clearing rates by maximum auction rate. Until right before the week of February 12, 2008, there was no statistical difference in clearing rates between bonds with high and low maximum auction rates. Since then, major auction dealers withdrew liquidity support and the ARS clearing rates became bifurcated by the maximum auction rate. That is, the clearing rates on bonds with high maximum auction rates had been significantly higher than those on bonds with low maximum auction rates.

The positive relationship between the auction clearing rate and the maximum auction rate clearly indicates that the post-crisis auctions are not competitive. The reason is that in a competitive equilibrium, bonds with auctions less likely to fail should require, all else being equal, lower interest rates to compensate for their lower liquidity risk. But we found earlier that bonds with high maximum auction rates have significantly lower likelihood to experience IDS. Thus, if auctions were competitive, bonds with high maximum rates would have lower reset rates. However, this puzzling positive relationship is consistent with the predictions of existing auction theories. As we discussed earlier, auction theories predict that without dealers' liquidity support, the reset rates may be arbitrarily close to maximum auction rates.

Besides maximum auction rates, other auction design characteristics also mattered more when auction dealers stopped making the market. Both reset frequency and minimum bidding size continue to be statistically significant but with larger coefficients.

Interestingly, reset rates are positively related to the liquidity in the non-auction secondary market in post-crisis auctions. The coefficient on the average daily number of non-auction trades is positive and statistically significant. The point estimate implies that reset rates increase 53 basis points for one additional trade per day in the interauction period prior to the current auction. This finding indicates that the existence of a more liquid non-auction secondary market may induce more aggressive bidding in noncompetitive auctions. This result casts doubt on the conventional notion that better secondary-market liquidity is universally good. Liquidity, combined with no dealers making markets, may have an unintended negative effect by altering the strategic behavior of bidders toward less-competitive bidding.

Finally, some key factors for ARS valuations changed dramatically after auction dealers stopped making markets. Notably, underlying ratings became more important. The difference between AA- and A-rated bonds widened in the post-crisis period. Reset rates on bonds rated AA or better and on A-rated bonds are, respectively, about 192 and 64 basis points lower than those on unrated bonds. These findings indicate that as investors became increasingly concerned about insurers' financial strength, they started to differentiate underlying ratings more.

4.4 The Fragility of Discretionary Liquidity Provision

We now turn to the question, what caused auction dealers to withdraw their liquidity support? In particular, why did major dealers do so at almost the same time? In this section, we show evidence that implicit liquidity support is vulnerable to systemic shocks and that, because of reputational externalities, coordination failures occurred among major auction dealers.

4.4.1 Single Dealer Problem

Let us first put aside possible strategic interactions among major dealers by assuming that the value of one dealer's reputation is independent of the actions of other dealers.

Predictions of the Theory of Implicit Contract

The theory of implicit contract suggests that discretionary liquidity support may be a feature of the optimal contract when reputation matters. In such a setting, the liquidity provider may withdraw support in order to preserve its financial capital when its own survival is under threat. For example, Boot et al. (1993) show that the use of legally unenforceable, discretionary financial contracts may be viable when reputation is valuable. In such a contract, when the promisor is hit by a negative shock, it may decide not to honor the implicit guarantee and forfeit its reputational capital in order to preserve its financial capital. Also, Gorton and Souleles (2006) show that in a setting with repeated financial contracting, a

24

sponsor may implicitly commit to "bail out" an off-balance-sheet special purpose vehicle (SPV) when the SPV would otherwise fail. Based on the value of reputation in obtaining future business, the implicit support mitigates the concerns over moral hazard and adverse selection. When the SPV is profitable, the sponsor uses it to subsidize its on-balance-sheet assets. However, when a bailout of the SPV would threaten the survival of the sponsor, the sponsor would let the SPV fail. This outcome most likely occurs when systemic shocks hit both on- and off-balance-sheet assets.

Reputation is valuable in the ARS market, as auction dealers are frequently the underwriters of ARS at issuance and have ongoing business relationships with the issuers. Loss of reputation or credibility caused by failed auctions may threaten dealers' underwriting business. In addition, many of the ARS investors are clients of the dealers' wealth management desks. Lack of liquidity in these markets may result in losing these clients.

Therefore, the theory of implicit contract predicts that auction dealers may keep making markets until preserving financial capital becomes critical to their own survival. In addition, a corollary of this cost-benefit analysis is that when auction dealers do make markets, they may require additional interest payments to compensate them for their funding costs. To seek supporting evidence for this theory, we first examined the dynamics of dealers' inventories and funding costs leading up to the ARS market collapse. We then tested whether auction clearing rates are positively related to dealers' funding costs when they do provide bidding support.

Dealer Inventory and Funding Costs

Figure 13 plots aggregate inventory accumulated by all dealers since January 1, 2007 (solid line). The series is estimated by adding up daily net dealer buys over all bonds. Aggregate inventory stayed largely unchanged in the first quarter of 2007. However, dealers started to aggressively pare down their inventories in the second quarter. The level of inventory picked up somewhat temporarily in the summer of 2007 when the financial market turmoil began, but it then fell again to reach its low toward the end of 2007. The sharp declines in aggregate inventory during the relatively quiet period in municipal bond markets are consistent with the predictions by Gorton and Souleles (2006). That is, dealers may have tried to free up capital from the ARS market to subsidize other parts of their balance sheets that were capital strained.

Aggregate ARS inventory rose sharply in late 2007 and early 2008. The concerns over monoline insurers intensified during this period, resulting in increased selling pressures in all parts of the municipal bond market. As auction dealers continued to make markets, they had to buy more in auctions but were not able to unload as much in the non-auction secondary market. The imbalance quickly drove dealers' inventories higher.

The increasing amount of capital required to support the auctions came at a time when major dealers strove to conserve their capital for their own survival. Concurrent with the rising ARS inventory, concerns heightened over the credit risk of major auction dealers. These concerns can be seen from the premiums of credit default swap contracts, which insure against dealer defaults. Figure 13 plots the average CDS spreads for the top 10 auction dealers (dashed line; ranked by market share). Major dealers' CDS spreads had been below 20 basis points through July 2007, but they rose to nearly 130 basis points on February 11 and continued to rise after that. Alternatively, because CDS spread is also an indicator of the cost of funds, the cost of raising an additional unit of capital increased substantially for major dealers.

Therefore, our analysis suggests that, consistent with the theory of implicit contracts, when auction dealers' own survival was a major concern, they stopped supporting the auctions and forfeited their reputational capital to preserve their financial capital.

Compensating Marketmaking Activities

We further tested whether auction clearing rates are positively related to the costs of making markets. The results are reported in table 7. In columns 1 and 3, we add only auction dealer CDS spreads in the regressions of auction clearing rates, and in columns 2 and 4, we add two more regressors: a dummy variable for pseudo failure (that is, when net dealer buys are positive) and its interactive term with dealer CDS spreads.

As we can see, compared with the results shown in table 6, including these additional regressors has little effect on the point estimates of other coefficients. In addition, in both the pre- and post-crisis periods, when adding only auction dealers' CDS spreads, their coefficients are not statistically significant (columns 1 and 3). However, in column 2, the coefficients on both the pseudo failure dummy variable and its interactive term with CDS spreads are statistically significant. That is, auction clearing rates are unrelated to auction dealers' funding costs when auctions are successful without dealers' support. But auction clearing rates are positively related to dealers' funding costs when dealers provide supporting bids. The magnitude of the dealer's influence on auction clearing rates is modest, though: Auction clearing rates increase about 6 basis points when the dealer's costs of funds rise 1 percentage point.

4.4.2 Multidealer Problem: Coordination Failure

The theory of implicit contracts is useful for understanding the average behavior of major auction dealers. But it cannot explain why all major auction dealers withdrew their liquidity support almost simultaneously. As shown later, there were wide variations across major dealers in the changes in their inventories and funding costs. Yet the timing of their withdrawal of liquidity support appeared to vary little. We argue that coordination failures in a reputation game among major dealers led to their simultaneous actions.

Evidence of Reputational Externality

A few major dealers dominated the MARS market. As shown in table 5, the top 10 auction dealers by market share made up nearly 95 percent of the market. In this multidealer setting, the value of one dealer's reputation may depend on the actions taken by other dealers. Reputation creates externality in the dealers' decisions on whether to support the auctions. In particular, being the first dealer to stop the liquidity support without others immediately following may be detrimental to the dealer's reputation. However, if many dealers act similarly at the same time, then the damage may be much smaller.

Indeed, the unwillingness to become the first mover may have kept the market going for a period of time. This reluctance is vividly depicted in a UBS internal e-mail in January 2008, in which its municipal finance director, David Schulman, described a worst case scenario as "contagion and reputational risk of UBS becoming first to fail and breaking the moral obligation to support these markets in an orderly fashion." Moreover, he further proposed to "continue to support all auctions" and stated that "if we do fail—be the 2nd to fail." (January 13, 2008, Exhibit 1, Massachusetts attorney general investigation).

The strategic complementarity leads to multiple equilibriums in the reputation game among dealers. Under certain market conditions, dealers will choose to continue to support the auctions if others also support their auctions, and they will withdraw if other dealers do the same. An all-support equilibrium, even if optimal globally, may not be stable. Small disturbances in some players' behavior will cause the whole game to move from the all-support equilibrium to the all-withdrawal equilibrium.

Unexpected First Mover

A key characteristic of the unravelling of the all-support equilibrium in the reputation game is the unpredictability of the first-mover; if the first mover is predictable, other dealers can coordinate to warn or help the potential first mover so that it does not defect. We show that to some extent the first overall withdrawal of liquidity support by Goldman Sachs was indeed unexpected.

Among major dealers, Goldman Sachs did not appear to have the most difficulty supporting its auctions. First, their overall implicit commitments were not the most onerous among all dealers. As shown in table 5, Goldman's market share was significantly lower than those of Citigroup, UBS, and Morgan Stanley and only modestly higher than those of other major dealers. Second, Goldman's remarketing effort had been more successful compared with such efforts of some other dealers. In fact, Goldman was able to pare down its inventory significantly over the course of 2007. On the eve of its overall withdrawal, Goldman's inventory was actually below its level at the beginning of 2007. Two other banks, UBS and the Royal Bank of Canada, had experienced more-significant inventory increases since 2007. Third, Goldman did not have the highest costs of capital. As a proxy for the costs of funds, CDS spreads on all major broker-dealers had increased significantly since July 2007. But spreads on Goldman were notably lower than those on Morgan Stanley and comparable with those on Citigroup. Both Morgan Stanley and Citigroup ranked higher in market share and experienced more inventory pressures, but neither indiscriminately withdrew its liquidity support before Goldman did.

In short, Goldman's move as the first one to abandon the market appeared to be unexpected. The unpredictable nature of the move and the visibility of Goldman may have triggered self-fulfilling responses by other dealers.

5 Conclusions and Policy Implications

The collapse of the ARS market in 2008 provides a unique laboratory for studying the role of discretionary liquidity provision during systemic events. We find that ARS auctions frequently drew insufficient investor demand, likely because of the fragmented nature of the market. In the pre-crisis period, the demand problem was solved by auction dealers acting as market markers. Such a market maker role is implicitly assumed without legal obligations. Even so, it has a significant effect on both net investor demand and auction clearing rates. In the pre-crisis period, when auction dealers supported the auctions, the likelihood of IDS was driven mostly by investors' exogenous liquidity shocks, and auction reset rates were strongly related to bond fundamental values and only weakly related to auction design factors. In the post-crisis period, after auction dealers stopped making markets, the likelihood of IDS depended not only on bond fundamentals but also heavily on auction design factors, most prominently maximum auction rates, to which this likelihood was strongly negatively related. In addition, consistent with the underpricing predictions of uniform-price auction theories, auction clearing rates deviated from fundamental values and were strongly positively related to maximum auction rates.

More importantly, we provide quantitative evidence that discretionary liquidity provision is fragile. First, auction dealers stopped making markets when their own survival was under threat. As auction dealers suffered losses from other financial markets, they forfeited their reputational capital in favor of preserving their financial capital. Second, reputational externality caused contagion among dealers in withdrawing liquidity supports, which exacerbated the fragility of implicit contracts.

The lessons we learn from the ARS market have broader implications. First, implicit liquidity support by dealers can be a source of systemic risk, because such support is likely to vanish precisely when dealers are suffering from losses in other financial markets. The withdrawal of such liquidity support resulted in the ARS market collapse. The collapse was not driven by the fundamental credit risk of the ARS issuers, because yield spreads on other comparable short-term municipal bonds did not rise around the time of the ARS crisis.

Second, implicit liquidity support is subject to contagion, in the sense that one dealer's decision to withdraw induces others to follow. In contrast, explicit contractual liquidity support would mitigate such risk, as dealers would no longer have a choice. This implication is important because the use of implicit liquidity support to facilitate maturity transformation is also a feature of many other markets. For example, structured investment vehicles in the asset-backed commercial paper market rely almost entirely on implicit liquidity support. Therefore, the lessons learned here can be generalized beyond the ARS market.

Third, our analysis draws attention to how regulations should treat implicit liquidity support for nonderivative products. Although the existing regulatory framework, such as Basel II, sets the guidance that derivative securities should move away from using implicit liquidity supports, no such guidance exists for cash securities such as ARS. Recent settlements of major broker-dealers with regulators required banks to buy back substantial amounts of ARS sold before the crisis, suggesting that non-contractual support should be treated as if it were contractual where capital requirements are concerned.

Importantly, our study does not necessarily imply that regulators should directly restrict the use of implicit contracts. The theory of implicit contracts suggests that, under certain conditions, implicit contracts are optimal and can also foster the growth of reputational capital, even if explicit contracts are enforceable (Boot et al., 1993). However, certain policy measures may help reduce the fragility of implicit contracts. For example, our research suggests that the lack of transparency may have created a false sense of safety among investors and may allow vulnerabilities to build. If investors had known that the auctions were so heavily supported, they might not have been so surprised when dealers did stop making markets. What is more, some might have decided that the small additional yield on ARS was not worth the risk.

References

Acharya, Viral V., Philipp Schnabl and Gustavo Suarez (2010), 'Securitization without risk transfer', NBER Working Paper, wp. 15730.

Alderson, Michael J. and Donald R. Fraser (1993), 'Financial innovations and excesses revisited: The case of auction rate preferred stock', *Financial Management* **22**(2), 61–75.

Alderson, Michael J., Keith C. Brown and Scott L. Lummer (1987), 'Dutch auction rate preferred stock', *Financial Management* **16**(2), 68–73.

Austin, D. Andrew (2008), 'Auction-rate securities', Congressional Research Service, Report RL34672, Government and Finance Division. http://wikileaks.org/wiki/CRS-RL34672.

Back, Kerry and Jaime F. Zender (1993), 'Auctions of divisible goods: On the rationale for the treasury experiment', *Review of Financial Studies* **6**(4), 733–764.

Back, Kerry and Jaime F. Zender (2001), 'Auctions of divisible goods with endogenous supply', *Economics Letters* **73**(1), 29–34.

Bergstresser, Daniel, Shawn Cole and Siddharth Shenai (2009), 'UBS and auction rate securities', Harvard Business School Case Study: N9-209-093. HBS Case Study.

Bernanke, Ben S. (2009), 'Reflections on a year of crisis', Speech At the Federal Reserve Bank of Kansas City's Annual Economic Symposium, Jackson Hole, Wyoming. Also delivered at the Brookings Institution's Conference on "A Year of Turmoil," on September 15, 2009.

Boot, Arnoud, Stuart Greenbaum and Anjan V. Thakor (1993), 'Reputation and discretion in financial contracting', *American Economic Review* **83**(5), 1165–1183.

Brunnermeier, Markus K. (2009), 'Deciphering the liquidity and credit crunch 2007-2008.', *Journal of Economic Perspectives* **23**(1), 77–100.

Brunnermeier, Markus K. and Lasse Heje Pedersen (2009), 'Market liquidity and funding liquidity.', *Review of Financial Studies* **22**(6), 2201–2238.

Calomiris, Charles W and Charles M Kahn (1991), 'The role of demandable debt in structuring optimal banking arrangements', *American Economic Review* **81**(3), 497–513.

Calomiris, Charles W. and Joseph R. Mason (2003), 'Fundamentals, panics, and bank distress during the depression', *American Economic Review* **93**(5), 1615–1647.

Campbell, John Y., Andrew W. Lo and A. Craig MacKinlay (1997), *The Econometrics of Financial Markets*, Princeton University Press.

Cass, David and Karl Shell (1983), 'Do sunspots matter?', *Journal of Political Economy* **91**(2), 193–227.

Comerton-Forde, Carole, Terrence Hendershott, Charles M. Jones, Pamela C. Moulton and Mark S. Seasholes (2010), 'Time variation in liquidity: The role of market-maker inventories and revenues.', *Journal of Finance* **65**(1), 295 – 331.

Comment, Robert (2010), 'A note on the disposition of auctionrate securities by nonfinancial corporate investors', The Johns Hopkins Carey Business School Working Paper.

Commonwealth of Massachusetts (2008), 'Administrative complaint, in the matter of UBS securities, LLC and UBS financial services, Inc', Docket No. 2008-0045. Securities Division, Office of the Secretary of the Commonwealth.

Covitz, Daniel, Nellie Liang and Gustavo Suarez (2009), 'The anatomy of a financial crisis: The evolution of runs in the asset-backed commercial paper market', Working paper, Federal Reserve Board.

Damianov, Damian S. (2005), 'Erratum to 'the uniform price auction with endogenous supply", *Economics Letters* **89**(1), 133.

De Bandt, Olivier and Philipp Hartmann (2002), Systemic risk: A survey, *in* C.Goodhart and G.Illing, eds, 'Financial Crisis, Contagion and the Lender of Last Resort: A Book of Readings', Oxford University Press, pp. 249–298.

Detragiache, Enrica, Paolo Garella and Luigi Guiso (2000), 'Multiple versus single banking relationships: Theory and evidence.', *Journal of Finance* **55**(3), 1133–1161.

Diamond, Douglas and Philip H. Dybvig (1983), 'Bank runs, deposit insurance and liquidity', *Journal of Political Economy* **91**, 401–419.

Diamond, Douglas W. and Raghuram G. Rajan (2001), 'Liquidity risk, liquidity creation, and financial fragility: A theory of banking', *Journal of Political Economy* **109**(2), 287–327.

Froot, Ken (2009), 'Vicious cycles, investor behavior, and dealer-based financial systems', Harvard Business School Working Paper.

Goldstein, Michael A. and Edith S. Hotchkiss (2007), 'Dealer behavior and the trading of newly issued corporate bonds', AFA 2009 San Francisco Meetings Paper.

Gorton, Gary (1985), 'Bank suspension of convertibility', *Journal of Monetary Economics* **15**(2), 177–193.

Gorton, Gary (1988), 'Banking panics and business cycles', *Oxford Economic Papers* **40**, 751–81.

Gorton, Gary and Andrew Metrick (2009), 'Securitized banking and the run on repo', NBER.

Gorton, Gary and Nicholas S. Souleles (2006), *The Risks of Financial Institutions*, University of Chicago, chapter Special Purpose Vehicles and Securitization. Edited by Rene Stulz and Mark Carey.

Green, Richard C. (1993), 'A simple model of the taxable and tax-exempt yield curve', *Review of Financial Studies* **6**(2), 233–264.

Green, Richard C., Burton Hollifield and Norman Schurhoff (2007*a*), 'Dealer intermediation and price behavior in the aftermarket for new bond issues.', *Journal of Financial Economics* **86**(3), 643 – 682.

Green, Richard C., Burton Hollifield and Norman Schurhoff (2007*b*), 'Financial intermediation and the costs of trading in an opaque market.', *Review of Financial Studies* **20**(2), 275 – 314.

Jacklin, C. and Sudipto Bhattacharya (1988), 'Distinguishing panics and information based bank runs: Welfare and policy implications', *Journal of Political Economy* **96**(3), 568–92.

LiCalzi, Marco and Alessandro Pavan (2005), 'Tilting the supply schedule to enhance competition in uniform-price auctions', *European Economic Review* **49**(1), 227–250.

MacLeod, W. Bentley (2007), 'Reputations, relationships, and contract enforcement.', *Journal of Economic Literature* **45**(3), 595 – 628.

McAdams, David (2007), 'Adjustable supply in uniform price auctions: Non-commitment as a strategic tool', *Economics Letters* **95**(1), 48–53.

McConnell, John J. and Alessio Saretto (2010), 'Auction failures and the market for auction rates securities', *Journal of Financial Economics* **97**(3), 451–469.

Shin, Hyun Song (2009), 'Reflections on northern rock: The bank run that heralded the global financial crisis.', *Journal of Economic Perspectives* **23**(1), 101–119.

SIFMA (2007), 'Best practices for broker-dealers of auction rate securities', http://www.sifma.org/services/pdf/AuctionRateSecurities_FinalBestPractices.pdf. Securities Industry and Financial Markets Association.

Wang, James J. D. and Jaime F. Zender (2002), 'Auctioning divisible goods', *Economic Theory* **19**(4), 673–705.

Wilson, R. (1979), 'Auctions of shares', *Quarterly Journal of Economics* **93**, 675–698.

Winkler, Daniel T. and George B. Flanigan (1991), 'Default risk premia in the near-cash investment market: The case of auction rate preferred stock versus commercial paper', *Journal of Financial Research* **14**(4), 337–343.

Table 1: **Sample Construction**

To construct our sample, we start with all ARS contained in auction reports received from Wilmington Trust (WT), Bank of New York Mellon (BNYM), and Deutsche Bank (DB) and impose a set of restrictions to filter out bonds that are not municipal securities or have missing values for key variables. This table shows how the sample changes after each filtering.

Sampling	Number of bonds
1. All ARS from WT, BNYM, and DB	4,945
2. Municipal securities appearing in MSRB's transaction report	3,709
3. Having Bloomberg bond description data	3,567
4. 7 Days $\leq$ reset frequencies $\leq$ 35 days	3,526 ("overall sample")
5. Maximum-rate rules are identified	2,845 ("restricted sample")

Table 2: **Summary Statistics**

	Whole sample, $N = 3,526$		Restricted sample,[a] $N = 2,845$	
	Panel A: Categorical Variables			
	N	Percent	N	Percent
Is student loan	1,063	30.2	688	24.2
Is a GO bond	51	1.5	50	1.8
Is taxable	605	17.2	406	14.3
Reset period				
7	1,600	45.4	1,418	49.8
14	3	0.1	3	0.1
21	1	0.0	0	0.0
28	631	17.9	458	16.1
35	1,291	36.6	966	34.0
Underlying rating				
AAA	4	0.1	3	0.1
AA	576	16.3	522	18.3
A	1,181	33.5	1,034	36.3
BBB	302	8.6	255	8.9
Unrated	1,463	41.5	1,031	36.2
Strength of bond insurers[b]				
Strong	388	11.0	363	12.7
Weak	1,468	41.4	1,174	41.2
Other insurers	690	19.5	606	21.1
Not insured	945	27.9	671	23.6
Multiple Re-marketing Agents	994	28.0	814	28.5
Top 5 auction dealers	2,285	64.7	1,770	64.7
Citigroup	762	21.6	639	22.4
UBS	648	18.4	487	17.6
Morgan Stanley	356	10.1	294	10.3
RBC	278	7.9	198	6.9
Goldman Sachs	241	6.8	228	8.0
	Panel B: Continuous Variables			
	Mean	Std. Dev.	Mean	Std. Dev.
Bond size($ MM)	53.6	39.7	53.5	29.2
Minimum bid size ($ K)	39.8	26.3	38.4	26.4
Remaining years-to-maturity	23.7	8.1	23.6	8.1
N. of non-auction trades per day	0.38	0.64	0.39	0.66
N. of auction trades per auction	9.62	13.4	9.99	13.9

[a]The restricted sample excludes bonds for which we are unable to determine their maximum rates.

[b]Strong insurers are FSA and Assured Guaranty; and weak insurers are those under review for downgrades and in the headline news, including Ambac, MBIA, FGIC, CFIG, and XLCA.

Table 3: **Maximum Auction Rates**

Panel A shows the distribution of the types of maximum rate rules. Broadly speaking, there are fixed and floating rules, whereas among floating rules, they may be multiplicative, additive, or complex. Our definitions of these types are the following:

- Fixed: maximum rate is fixed at a number, say 15 percent;
- Multiplicative: maximum rate is a multiple of a benchmark rate up to a fixed cap rate;
- Additive: maximum rate is equal to a markup plus a benchmark rate up to a fixed cap rate;
- Complex: complex formula, usually with a mix of multiplicative and additive formulas and often linking to interest payments made during a period of time prior to the current auction.

Panel B shows summary statistics of maximum rates for the restricted sample. They are computed for all bond-dates because, for bonds with floating maximum-rate rules, maximum rates may change for each auction.

Panel A: Types of maximum-rate rules				Floating Rules		
Sample	Fixed	Floating	Total	Multiplicative	Additive	Complex
Auctions never failed	865	106	971	49	5	52
Auctions failed only once	191	141	332	136	4	1
Auctions failed twice or more	87	1,455	1,542	1,219	141	95
Total	1,143	1,702	2,845	1,404	150	148
Panel B: Summary Statistics of Maximum Rates						
Mean	13.9	6.85	10.4	6.94	6.37	6.06
(Std. dev.)	(1.75)	(1.98)	(3.99)	(2.05)	(1.23)	(1.14)

Data sources: Auction agents, Bloomberg, and authors' compilations.

Table 4: Determinants of Investor Demand Shortfall

This table shows the results from probit regressions of the likelihood of investor demand shortfall (IDS) for both pre- and post-crisis periods. IDS is a dummy variable that takes the value one if there is either an actual auction failure or positive net dealer buy in the auction. Standard errors, shown in parentheses, are clustered at the issuer level. * and ** indicate that the corresponding p-values are less than 0.10 and 0.05, respectively.

	pre-crisis, 7/1/07-12/31/07				post-crisis, 2/27/08-3/19/08			
	(1)	(2)	(3)	(4)	(5)	(6)	(7)	(8)
	Coeff/SE	Coeff/SE	Coeff/SE	Marg. Eff.	Coeff/SE	Coeff/SE	Coeff/SE	Marg. Eff.
Log(size)	0.251**	0.247**	0.252**	0.099**	0.104*	0.121**	0.124**	0.024**
	(0.02)	(0.02)	(0.02)	(0.01)	(0.06)	(0.06)	(0.06)	(0.01)
Log(maturity)	0.013	0.013	0.010	0.004	0.072	0.078	0.113	0.022
	(0.03)	(0.03)	(0.03)	(0.01)	(0.10)	(0.10)	(0.08)	(0.02)
Log(bond age)	-0.047**	-0.047**	-0.022	-0.009	0.568**	0.548**	0.158**	0.031**
	(0.01)	(0.01)	(0.02)	(0.01)	(0.04)	(0.05)	(0.05)	(0.01)
Is taxable	-0.238**	-0.245**	-0.270**	-0.107**	0.005	-0.044	0.449**	0.072**
	(0.07)	(0.07)	(0.07)	(0.03)	(0.16)	(0.16)	(0.13)	(0.02)
Refunding bond	-0.038	-0.038	-0.037	-0.015	-0.049	-0.039	-0.069	-0.014
	(0.03)	(0.03)	(0.03)	(0.01)	(0.09)	(0.09)	(0.06)	(0.01)
Is student loan	0.143*	0.150*	0.200**	0.077**	1.983**	1.913**	1.628**	0.169**
	(0.08)	(0.09)	(0.09)	(0.03)	(0.33)	(0.34)	(0.37)	(0.01)
Is GO bond	-0.127	-0.126	-0.088	-0.035	0.175	0.170	-0.143	-0.031
	(0.08)	(0.08)	(0.08)	(0.03)	(0.24)	(0.24)	(0.22)	(0.05)
Strong insurers	-0.000	0.001	0.006	0.002	-0.116	-0.077	0.277	0.049*
	(0.07)	(0.07)	(0.07)	(0.03)	(0.24)	(0.24)	(0.18)	(0.03)
Weak insurers	0.019	0.021	0.023	0.009	0.101	0.138	0.488**	0.094**
	(0.07)	(0.07)	(0.07)	(0.03)	(0.23)	(0.23)	(0.17)	(0.03)
Other insurers	0.062	0.063	0.046	0.018	0.000	0.035	0.451**	0.078**
	(0.07)	(0.07)	(0.07)	(0.03)	(0.23)	(0.23)	(0.17)	(0.03)
Underly. rat. $\geq$ AA	-0.091*	-0.092*	-0.083*	-0.033*	-0.173	-0.158	-0.262**	-0.056*
	(0.05)	(0.05)	(0.05)	(0.02)	(0.14)	(0.14)	(0.13)	(0.03)
Underly. rat. = A	-0.044	-0.043	-0.045	-0.018	-0.159	-0.159	-0.184	-0.037
	(0.05)	(0.05)	(0.05)	(0.02)	(0.13)	(0.13)	(0.11)	(0.02)
Underly. rat. $\leq$ BBB	0.059	0.062	0.050	0.020	-0.101	-0.120	-0.007	-0.001
	(0.07)	(0.07)	(0.06)	(0.02)	(0.17)	(0.17)	(0.15)	(0.03)
Muni 1-year index	0.455**	0.454**	0.435**	0.171**	0.032	0.040	0.348	0.069
	(0.10)	(0.10)	(0.10)	(0.04)	(0.19)	(0.19)	(0.25)	(0.05)
Muni term spread	0.776**	0.773**	0.771**	0.303**	-0.092	-0.095	0.430	0.085
	(0.10)	(0.10)	(0.10)	(0.04)	(0.61)	(0.61)	(0.77)	(0.15)
Vol. of swap rate	0.010*	0.010*	0.009	0.003	0.002	0.001	-0.006	-0.001
	(0.01)	(0.01)	(0.01)	(0.00)	(0.01)	(0.01)	(0.01)	(0.00)
Log(reset freq)		-0.003	0.006	0.002		0.283**	0.237**	0.047**
		(0.03)	(0.03)	(0.01)		(0.06)	(0.06)	(0.01)
Min. piece (K)		0.000	0.001	0.000		-0.002	-0.003*	-0.001
		(0.00)	(0.00)	(0.00)		(0.00)	(0.00)	(0.00)
Lag. non-auc. trade		0.043*	0.039	0.015		-0.136*	0.055	0.011
		(0.03)	(0.03)	(0.01)		(0.07)	(0.07)	(0.01)
Maximum rate			0.021**	0.008**			-0.223**	-0.044**
			(0.01)	(0.00)			(0.01)	(0.00)
Constant	-6.748**	-6.692**	-6.955**		-1.847	-2.654	-2.188	
	(0.63)	(0.63)	(0.63)		(2.06)	(2.07)	(2.27)	
Pseudo-R^2	0.02	0.02	0.02	0.02	0.19	0.19	0.43	0.43
N	32005	32005	32005	32005	5491	5491	5491	5491

Table 5: Abnormal Investor Demand Shortfalls upon the News of the Withdrawal of Liquidity Support by Major Auction Dealers

We estimate "abnormal" IDS in the two weeks after February 12, 2008 when major auction dealers reportedly withdrew their liquidity supports to the auctions. We first compute the predicted probability of IDS using the probit model of IDS estimated for 2/27/2008-3/19/2008, a period when it had become certain that all major dealers have stopped supporting the auctions. That is, $\hat{p}_{it} = E(\mathbf{I}_{it}|X_{it}) = 1 - \Phi(\hat{\beta}X_{it})$, where the indicator $\mathbf{I}_{it} = 1$ if IDS occurs, 0 otherwise. Then, we compute the abnormal IDS for bond i at t by $p_{it}^{\star} = \mathbf{I}_{it} - \hat{p}_{it}$. Let N_t be the number of bonds in auctions at t. At t, the observed rate of IDS is $\bar{p}_t = \frac{\sum_i \mathbf{I}_{it}}{N_t}$, the average predicted IDS rate is $\bar{\hat{p}}_t = \frac{\sum_i \hat{p}_{it}}{N_t}$, and the average abnormal IDS rate is $\overline{p^{\star}}_t = \frac{\sum_i p_{it}^{\star}}{N_t}$.

Date	$\bar{p}_t$	$\bar{\hat{p}}_t$	$\overline{p^{\star}}_t$	Std. Dev. of $p_{it}^{\star}$	N_t	t-Statistics of $\overline{p^{\star}}_t$
11-Feb-08	0.82	0.63	0.19	0.51	227	5.72
12-Feb-08	0.81	0.62	0.19	0.49	369	8.23
13-Feb-08	0.90	0.70	0.21	0.37	470	12.29
14-Feb-08	0.78	0.69	0.09	0.37	365	4.82
15-Feb-08	0.76	0.66	0.11	0.38	443	6.13
19-Feb-08	0.79	0.71	0.08	0.35	497	7.10
20-Feb-08	0.79	0.72	0.07	0.37	475	4.25
21-Feb-08	0.78	0.71	0.08	0.37	360	4.09
22-Feb-08	0.75	0.65	0.10	0.38	179	3.57
25-Feb-08	0.82	0.71	0.11	0.34	284	6.27
26-Feb-08	0.76	0.71	0.06	0.39	436	3.40
2/11-2/26	0.79	0.68	0.11	0.39	4105	18.64

Table 6: Determinants of Auction Clearing Rates

This table shows the results from OLS regressions of auction reset rates for the pre-crisis period from 7/1/2007 to 12/31/2007 and the post-crisis period from 2/27/2008 to 3/19/2008. Standard errors, shown in the parentheses, are clustered at the issuer level. * and ** indicate that the corresponding p-values are less than 0.10 and 0.05, respectively.

	pre-crisis 7/1/07-12/31/07		post-crisis 2/27/08-3/19/08	
	(1)	(2)	(3)	(4)
Log(size)	0.001	0.009	0.003	0.013
	(0.02)	(0.02)	(0.13)	(0.12)
Log(maturity)	0.021	0.032	0.317	0.265
	(0.03)	(0.02)	(0.21)	(0.19)
Log(bond age)	-0.010	-0.017*	0.156	0.046
	(0.01)	(0.01)	(0.11)	(0.10)
Is taxable	1.406**	1.364**	1.749**	1.337**
	(0.07)	(0.05)	(0.25)	(0.23)
Refunding bond	0.014	0.015	0.076	0.112
	(0.02)	(0.02)	(0.18)	(0.17)
Is student loan	0.565**	0.347**	-0.650	-0.459
	(0.07)	(0.06)	(1.21)	(1.02)
Is GO bond	-0.180**	-0.142**	-1.349**	-0.999**
	(0.05)	(0.04)	(0.34)	(0.37)
Strong insurers	-0.136**	-0.094*	1.789**	1.679**
	(0.06)	(0.05)	(0.32)	(0.30)
Weak insurers	-0.148**	-0.101**	2.560**	2.499**
	(0.06)	(0.05)	(0.31)	(0.29)
Other insurers	-0.064	-0.024	2.951**	2.884**
	(0.06)	(0.05)	(0.29)	(0.26)
Underly. rat. $\geq$ AA	-0.131**	-0.107**	-1.915**	-1.878**
	(0.04)	(0.03)	(0.34)	(0.32)
Underly. rat. = A	-0.068	-0.059	-0.639**	-0.568*
	(0.04)	(0.04)	(0.32)	(0.30)
Underly. rat. $\leq$ BBB	0.113**	0.091*	0.167	0.177
	(0.06)	(0.05)	(0.41)	(0.36)
Muni 1-year index	0.722**	0.717**	-0.570*	-0.547*
	(0.04)	(0.04)	(0.32)	(0.32)
Muni term spread	0.610**	0.615**	-0.056	0.764
	(0.03)	(0.03)	(1.38)	(1.47)
Vol. of swap rate	0.072**	0.071**	0.016	0.015
	(0.00)	(0.00)	(0.01)	(0.01)
Log(reset freq)		0.237**		0.594**
		(0.02)		(0.15)
Min. piece (K)		0.001**		0.008**
		(0.00)		(0.00)
Lag. non-auc. trade		-0.017		0.527**
		(0.01)		(0.15)
Maximum rate		0.012**		0.143**
		(0.00)		(0.04)
Constant	-0.628	-1.498**	5.504	-0.018
	(0.46)	(0.38)	(4.73)	(4.66)
R^2	0.63	0.66	0.27	0.32
N	31991	31991	2320	2320

Table 7: Dealer's Role in Determining Auction Clearing Rates

This table shows the results from OLS regressions of auction reset rates for the pre-crisis period from 7/1/2007 to 12/31/2007 and the post-crisis period from 2/27/2008 to 3/19/2008. Standard errors, shown in the parentheses, are clustered at the issuer level. * and ** indicate that the corresponding p-values are less than 0.10 and 0.05, respectively.

	pre-crisis 7/1/07-12/31/07		post-crisis 2/27/08-3/19/08	
	(1)	(2)	(3)	(4)
Log(size)	0.009	0.001	0.019	0.011
	(0.02)	(0.02)	(0.12)	(0.12)
Log(maturity)	0.032	0.032	0.253	0.254
	(0.02)	(0.02)	(0.19)	(0.19)
Log(bond age)	-0.017*	-0.017*	0.045	0.041
	(0.01)	(0.01)	(0.10)	(0.10)
Is taxable	1.363**	1.370**	1.339**	1.329**
	(0.05)	(0.05)	(0.23)	(0.23)
Refunding bond	0.016	0.018	0.108	0.114
	(0.02)	(0.02)	(0.17)	(0.17)
Is student loan	0.356**	0.351**	-0.480	-0.491
	(0.06)	(0.05)	(1.05)	(1.03)
Is GO bond	-0.143**	-0.141**	-0.986**	-0.981**
	(0.05)	(0.05)	(0.38)	(0.36)
Strong insurers	-0.093*	-0.093*	1.677**	1.662**
	(0.05)	(0.05)	(0.29)	(0.29)
Weak insurers	-0.099**	-0.100**	2.492**	2.468**
	(0.05)	(0.05)	(0.28)	(0.28)
Other insurers	-0.022	-0.024	2.878**	2.853**
	(0.05)	(0.05)	(0.26)	(0.26)
Underly. rat. $\geq$ AA	-0.107**	-0.104**	-1.877**	-1.862**
	(0.03)	(0.03)	(0.32)	(0.32)
Underly. rat. = A	-0.060	-0.058	-0.565*	-0.554*
	(0.04)	(0.04)	(0.30)	(0.30)
Underly. rat. $\leq$ BBB	0.091*	0.089*	0.170	0.173
	(0.05)	(0.05)	(0.36)	(0.36)
Muni 1-year index	0.712**	0.698**	-0.551*	-0.563*
	(0.04)	(0.04)	(0.32)	(0.33)
Muni term spread	0.598**	0.569**	0.990	0.947
	(0.03)	(0.03)	(1.53)	(1.50)
Vol. of swap rate	0.071**	0.071**	0.015	0.016
	(0.00)	(0.00)	(0.01)	(0.01)
Log(reset freq)	0.236**	0.235**	0.605**	0.600**
	(0.02)	(0.02)	(0.15)	(0.15)
Min. piece (K)	0.001**	0.001**	0.008**	0.008**
	(0.00)	(0.00)	(0.00)	(0.00)
Lag. non-auc. trade	-0.018	-0.019	0.517**	0.511**
	(0.01)	(0.01)	(0.15)	(0.15)
Maximum rate	0.012**	0.012**	0.141**	0.141**
	(0.00)	(0.00)	(0.04)	(0.04)
Dealer CDS, percent	0.027	-0.003	-0.052	-0.097
	(0.02)	(0.03)	(0.09)	(0.09)
Pseudo-failure		0.046**		-0.103
		(0.02)		(0.20)
Dealer CDS*Pseudo-failure		0.060**		0.133
		(0.03)		(0.10)
Constant	-1.469**	-1.264**	-0.554	-0.245
	(0.38)	(0.38)	(4.70)	(4.67)
R^2	0.66	0.67	0.32	0.32
N	31991	31991	2320	2320

Table 8: **Unexpected First Mover**

This table shows the changes in inventory and costs of funds for the top 10 broker-dealers (ranked by market share). Market share accounts for the amount of face values of the bonds for which the dealer acts as the lead manager. Change in inventory is the accumulative net dealer buy (both on auction dates and in the non-auction secondary market) from December 31, 2006 to February 11, 2008. Market share and Inventory calculation is based on our sample. CDS spreads are quoted in basis points from Markit.

| Dealers | Market shares | | Inventory ($Bill) | | CDS spreads (bps) | | |
| | | | Change from | | Level on | Change from | |
	$Bill	Percent	7/2/07	1/2/07	2/11/08	7/2/07	1/2/07
1. Citigroup	43.6	23.2	2.09	-0.10	106	91	98
2. UBS	32.7	17.4	4.85	3.42	84	73	79
3. Morgan Stanley	19.0	10.1	-0.76	-1.88	152	115	130
4. RBC	13.6	7.2	1.14	1.02	45	36	35
5. Goldman Sachs	13.5	7.2	-0.04	-0.82	107	69	85
6. Lehman Brothers	12.7	6.7	0.56	-0.04	180	140	159
7. Bear Stearns	12.6	6.7	-0.98	-1.63	275	222	253
8. Merrill Lynch	10.1	5.4	0.11	-1.02	179	141	163
9. JP Morgan	10.1	5.3	-0.35	-1.39	80	60	65
10. Bank of America	9.4	5.0	-0.94	-1.65	82	67	73
11. Top 10	112.9	94.1	5.90	-3.89	128	101	114

Figure 1: **Gross Issuance of Municipal Auction Rate Securities**
The bar chart plots quarterly gross issuance of MARS, in billion dollars, from 1996 to 2008
(left scale). The solid line shows the time series of municipal bond term spread, the difference
between long-term and short-term municipal bond yields, in percent (right scale).

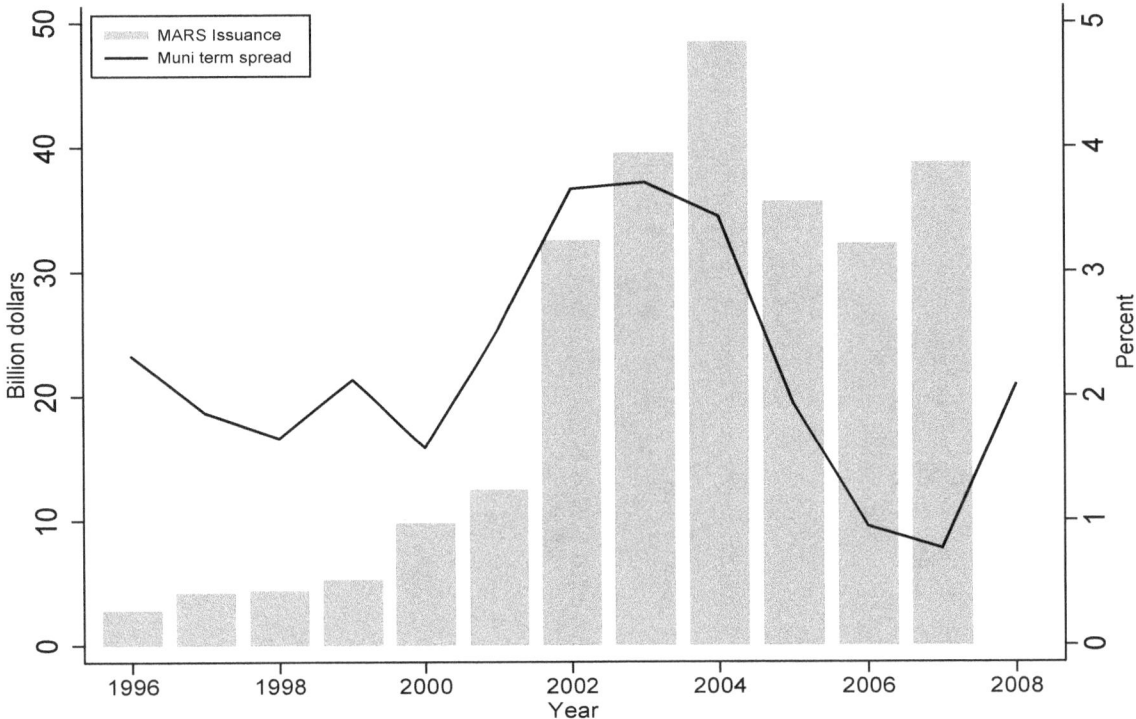

Figure 2: **The Auction Procedure**

This figure illustrates the auction process.

Auction Process

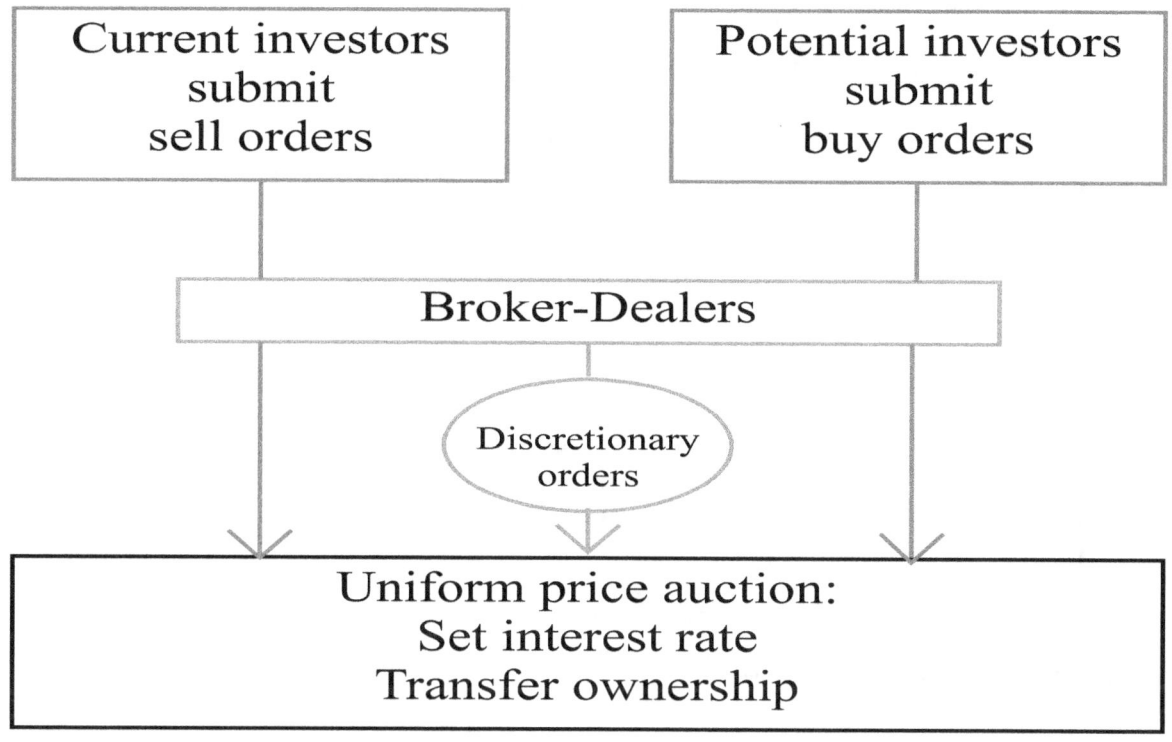

Note: Auctions take place in the secondary market.

Figure 3: **Distribution of Maximum Auction Rate by Maximum-Rate Rule**
This figure plots the histograms of maximum auction rates for MARS with floating maximum-rate rules (left panel) and with fixed maximum rate rules (right panel).

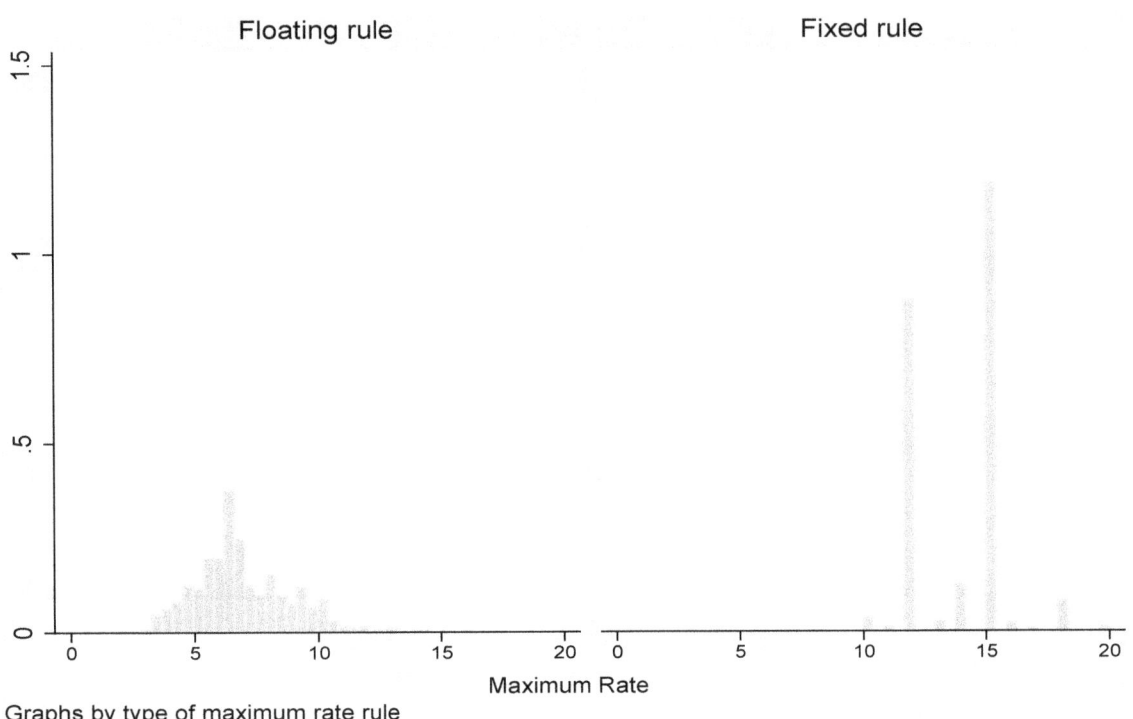

Graphs by type of maximum rate rule

Figure 4: **Gross and Net Buys by Auction Dealers in the MARS Auctions**
This figure shows the time series of average gross and net dealer buys per auction. Gross dealer buys equal total customer sells to dealers reported in the MSRB data on the auction dates, and net dealer buys equal total customer sells to dealers minus total customer buys from dealers reported in the MSRB data on the auction dates.

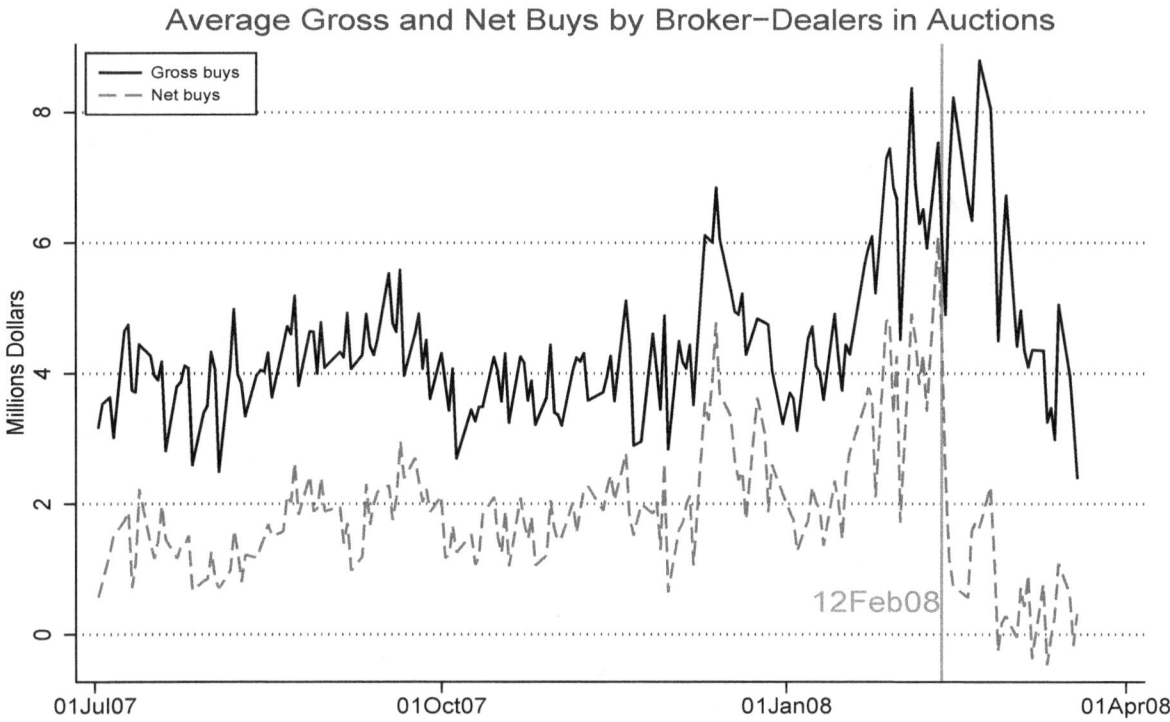

Figure 5: **Extent of Dealer Support in Successful Auctions in the Pre-Crisis Period**
This figure shows the distribution of the ratio of net dealer buys to gross dealer buys, conditional on non-zero gross dealer buys, among all successful auctions for the pre-crisis period between July 1, 2007 and December 31, 2007. In particular, a ratio of one corresponds to zero investor bid in the auction.

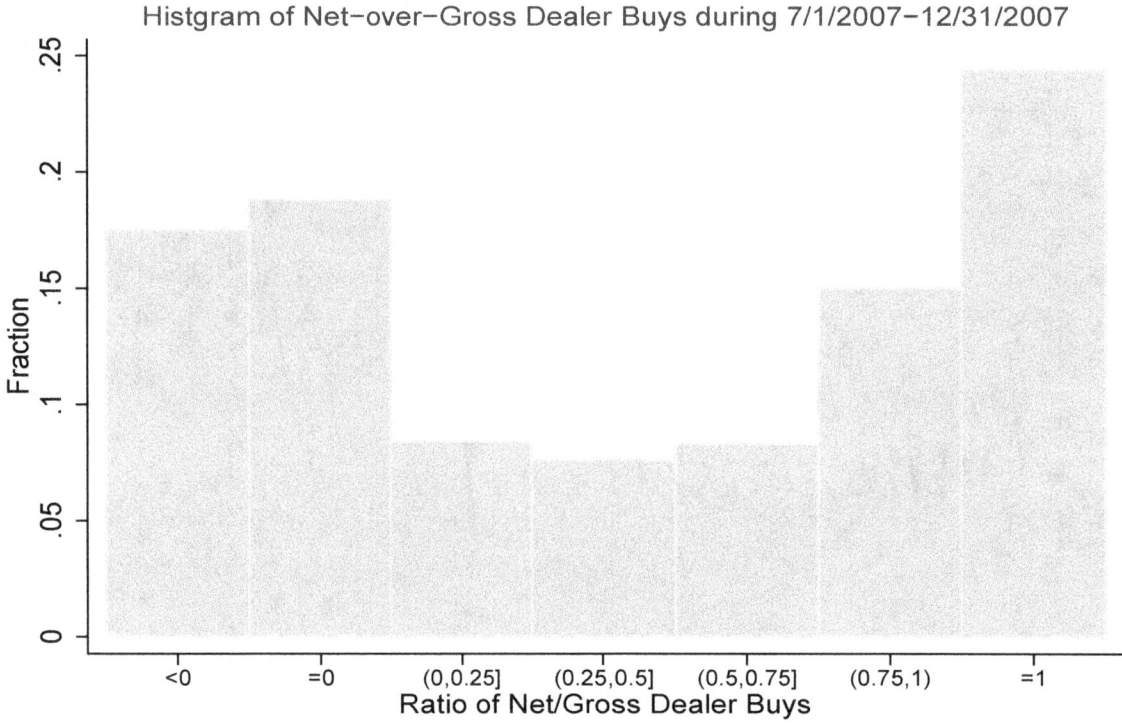

Figure 6: **Auction Dealers as Market Makers**

This figure shows average values of net dealer buys (in million dollars) per auction on the auction dates and in the inter-auction periods after auctions.

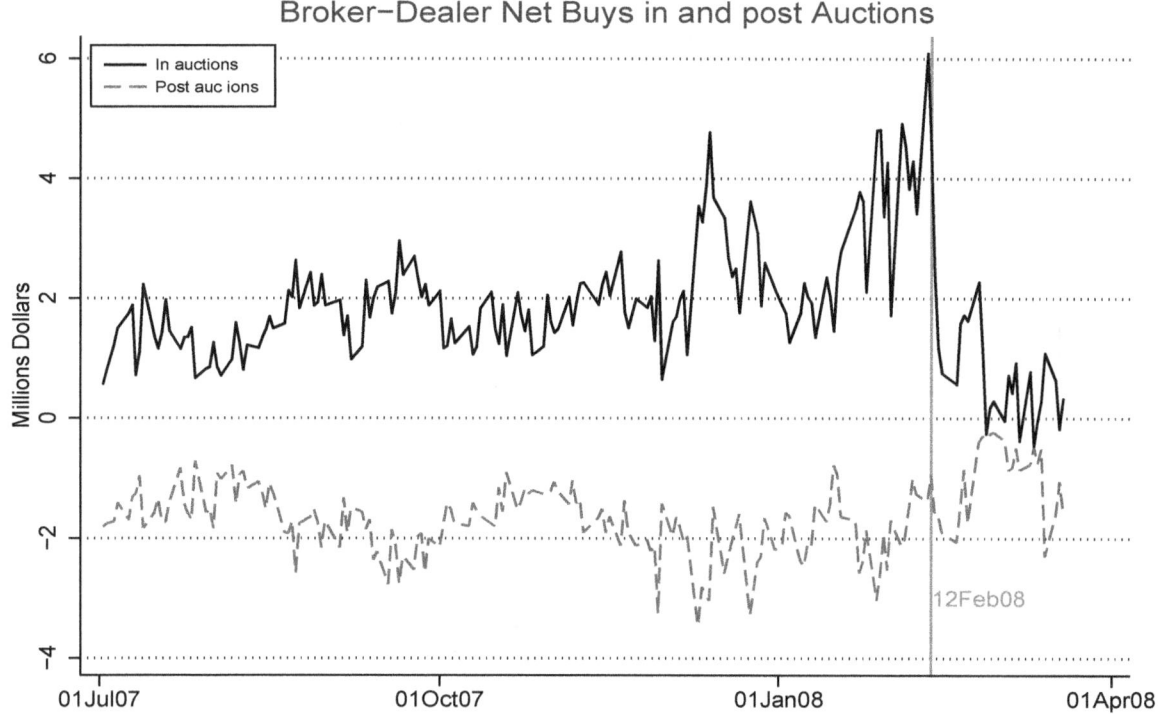

Figure 7: **The Rate of Actual Auction Failures by Major Auction Dealers**
This chart plots the percentage of MARS auctions in our sample that failed for each of the top 10 auction dealers (ranked by market share) in the week of February 11, 2008.

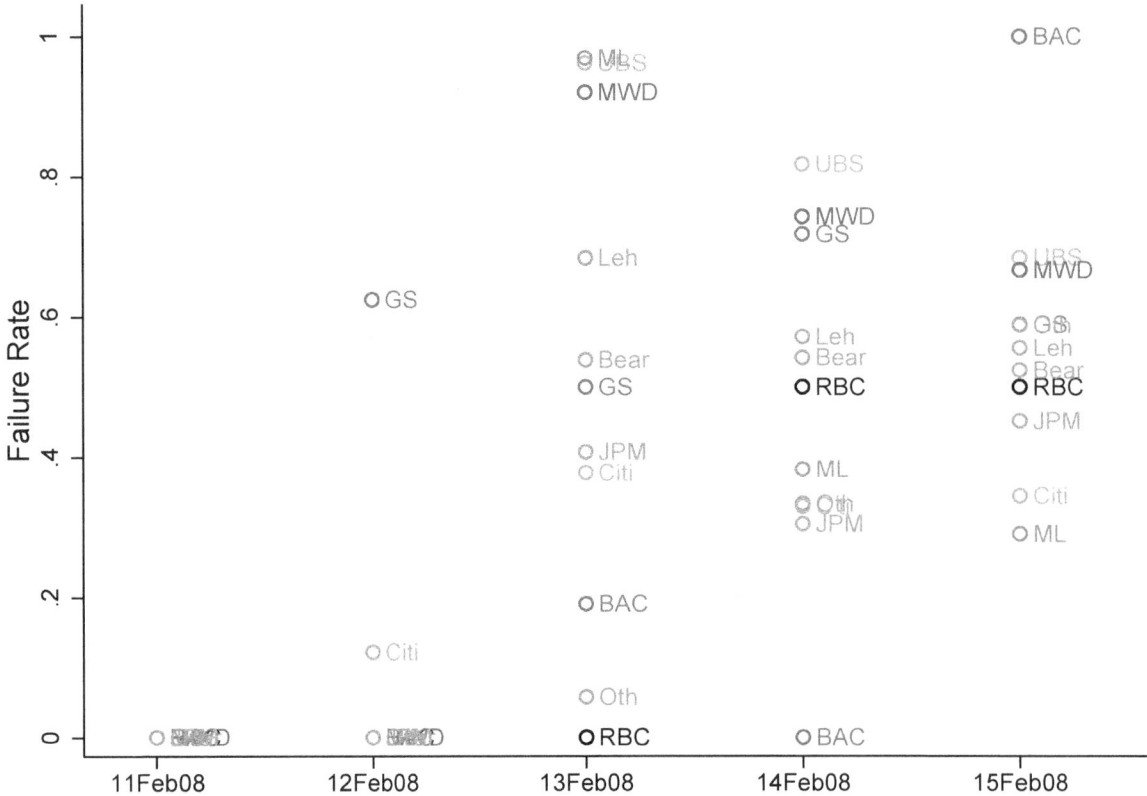

Figure 8: **The Rate of Investor Demand Shortfall**

This figure shows the time series of the fraction of auctions with investor demand shortfall (IDS). An IDS occurs when the total amount of buy orders by potential investors is less than the total amount of sell orders by existing bondholders. IDS can be inferred from either actual failure or pseudo failure. Pseudo failure refers to the case when the auction would have failed, had the dealer not placed supporting bids in the auction.

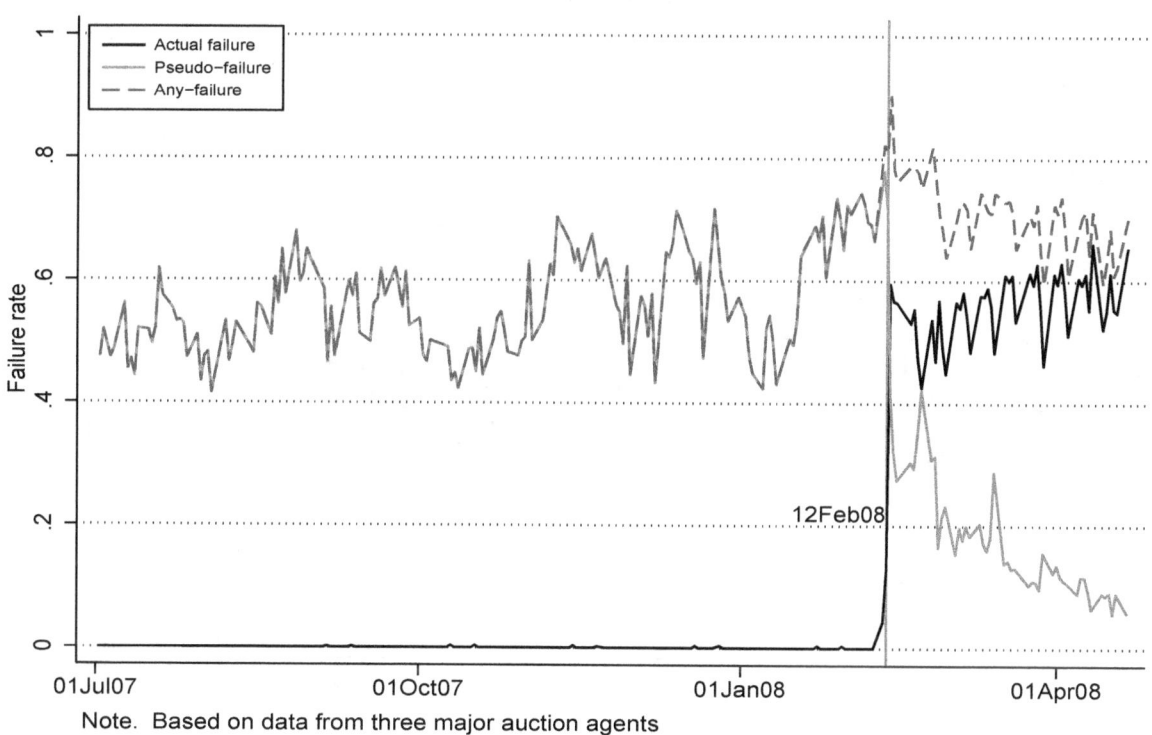

Note. Based on data from three major auction agents

49

Figure 9: **The Rate of Investor Demand Shortfall by Maximum Auction Rate**
This figure shows the time series of the fraction of auctions with investor demand shortfall by maximum auction rates. A maximum rate is classified as high if it is greater than 10 percent, otherwise it is low. The cutoff point, 10 percent, is about the median of maximum auction rates for all ARS in our sample.

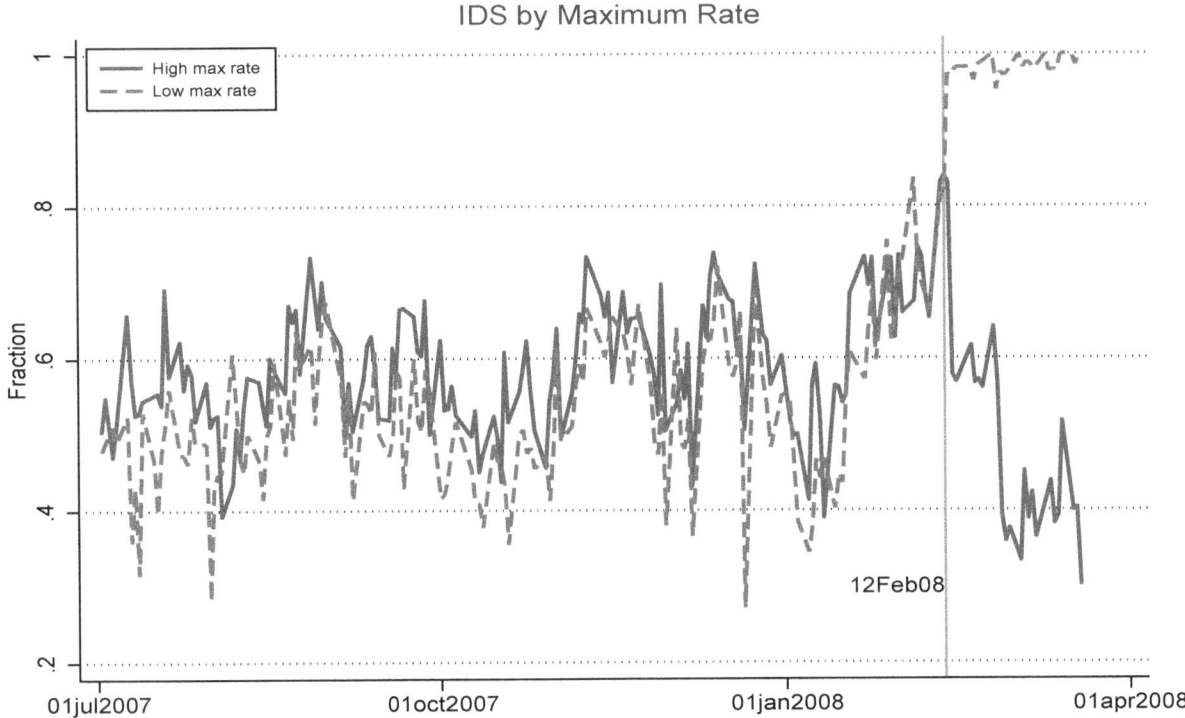

Figure 10: **Selected Results from Weekly Probit Regressions of Investor Demand Shortfall**

This figure shows the time series of pseudo-R^2 and the coefficients of maximum auction rates from the weekly probit regressions of investor demand shortfall. The empirical model is the same as in Table 4 except that the market condition variables, namely the one-year municipal bond rate, municipal yield term spread, and interest rate volatility, are excluded in the weekly regressions. The coefficients of other independent variables are available upon request.

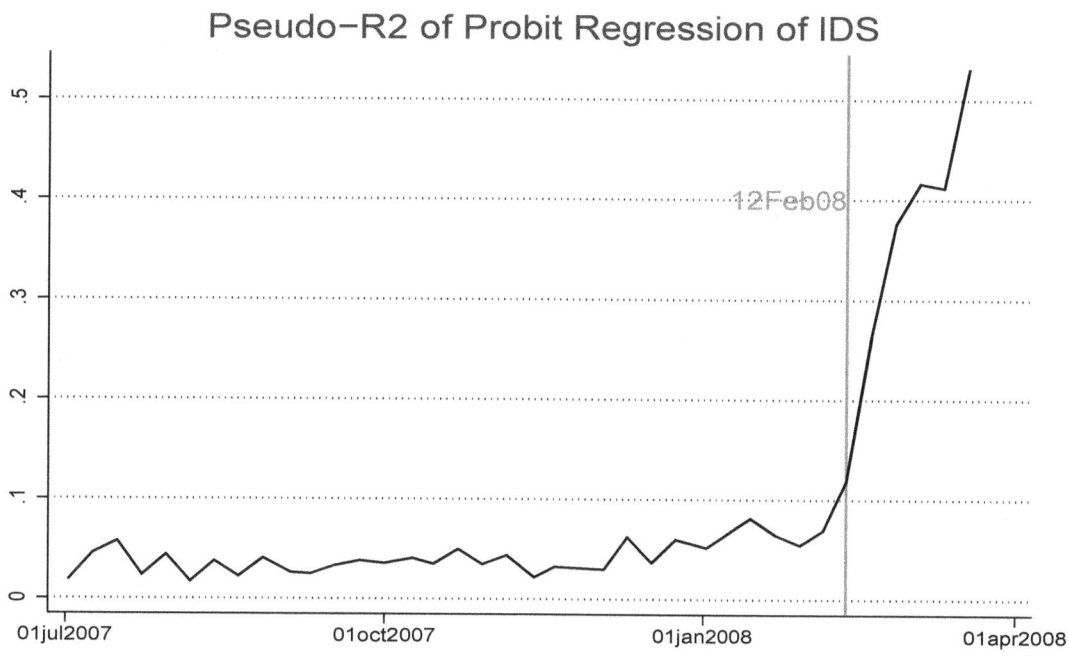

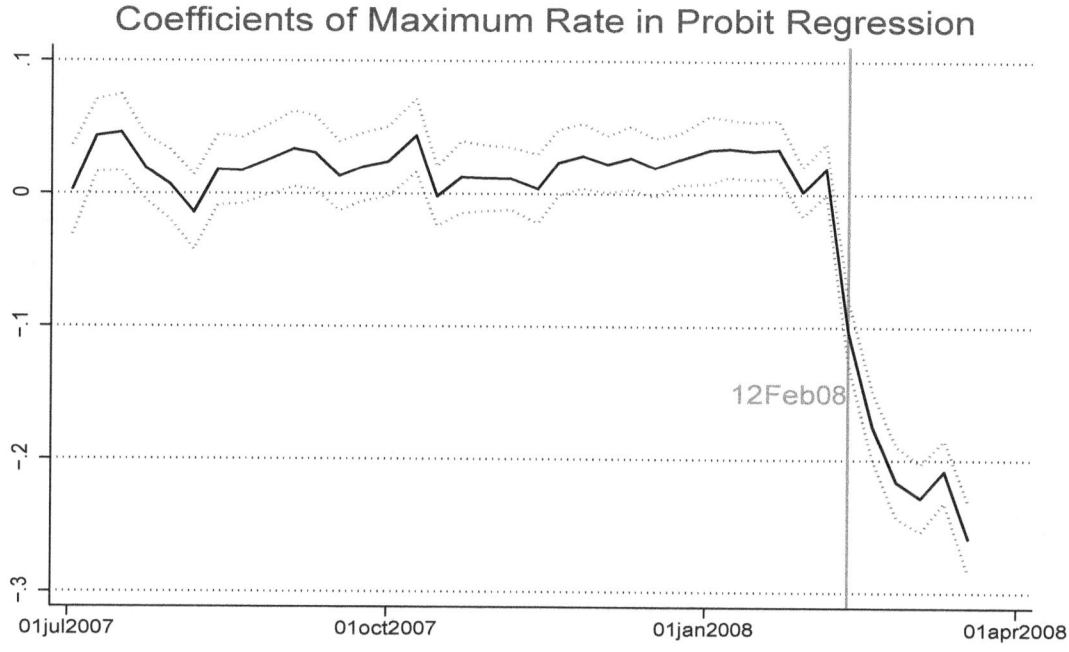

Figure 11: **The Ratios of Short-Term Municipal Bond Yields to Libor**
This figure shows the time series of the ratios of short-term municipal bond yields to one-month Libor. The short-term municipal bond rates include average auction clearing rates on ARS, the SIFMA 7-day swap rate index, and the one-year municipal bond yield from Municipal Market Advisor.

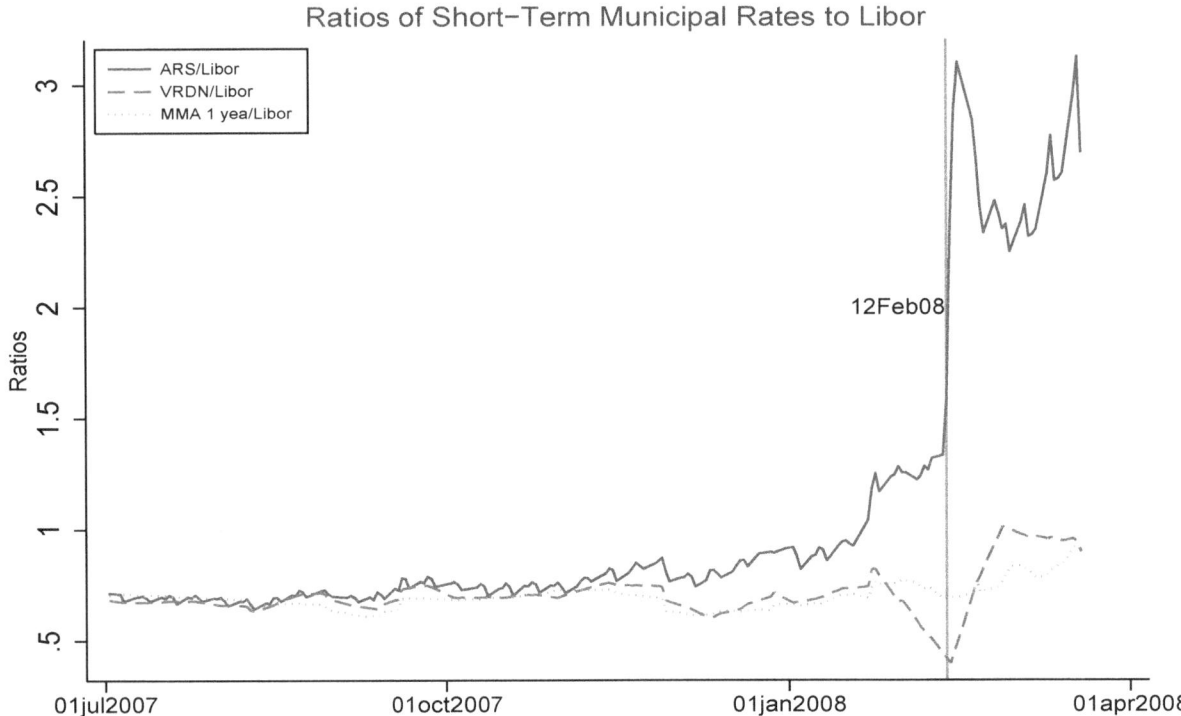

Figure 12: **The ARS Clearing Rates by Maximum Auction Rate**

This figure shows the time series of ARS auction clearing rates on successful auctions by maximum auction rate. A maximum rate is classified as high if it is greater than 10 percent, otherwise it is low. The cutoff point, 10 percent, is about the median of maximum auction rates for all ARS in our sample.

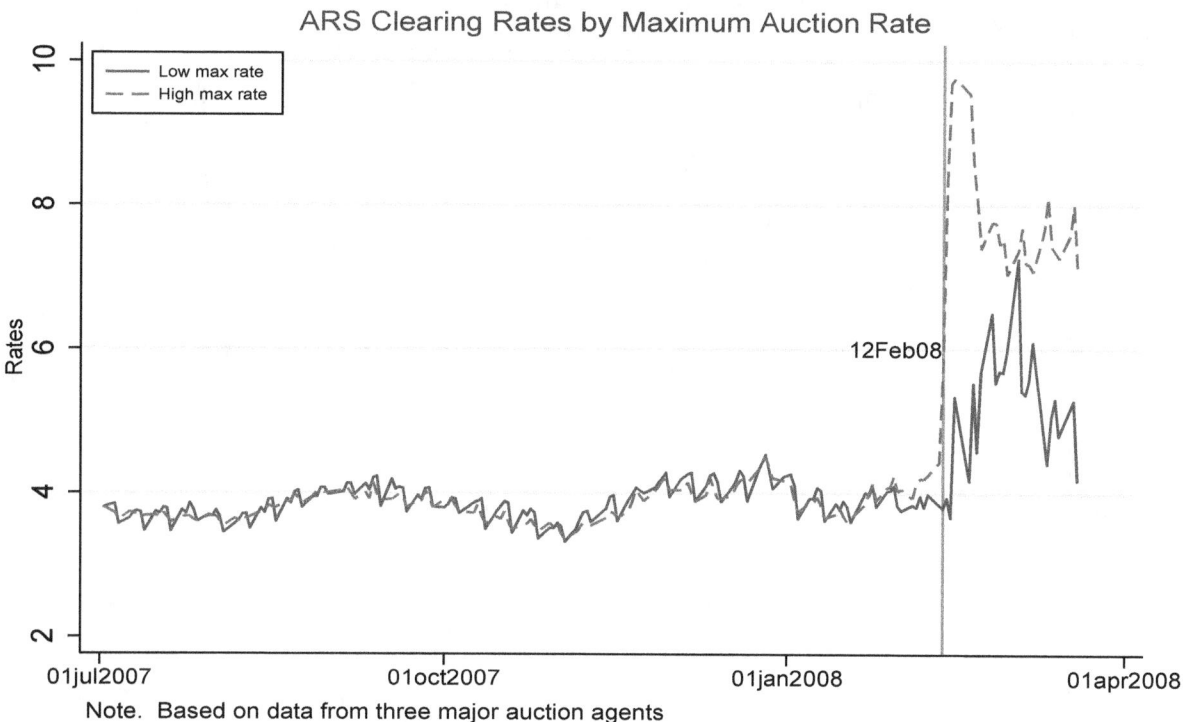

Figure 13: **Cumulative Inventory of All Auction Dealers**
This figure shows the total cumulative changes in all auction dealers' inventory since the beginning of 2007. Daily changes in dealers' inventories equal total "customer sell to dealers" minus total "customer buy from dealers" reported in the MSRB transactions data.

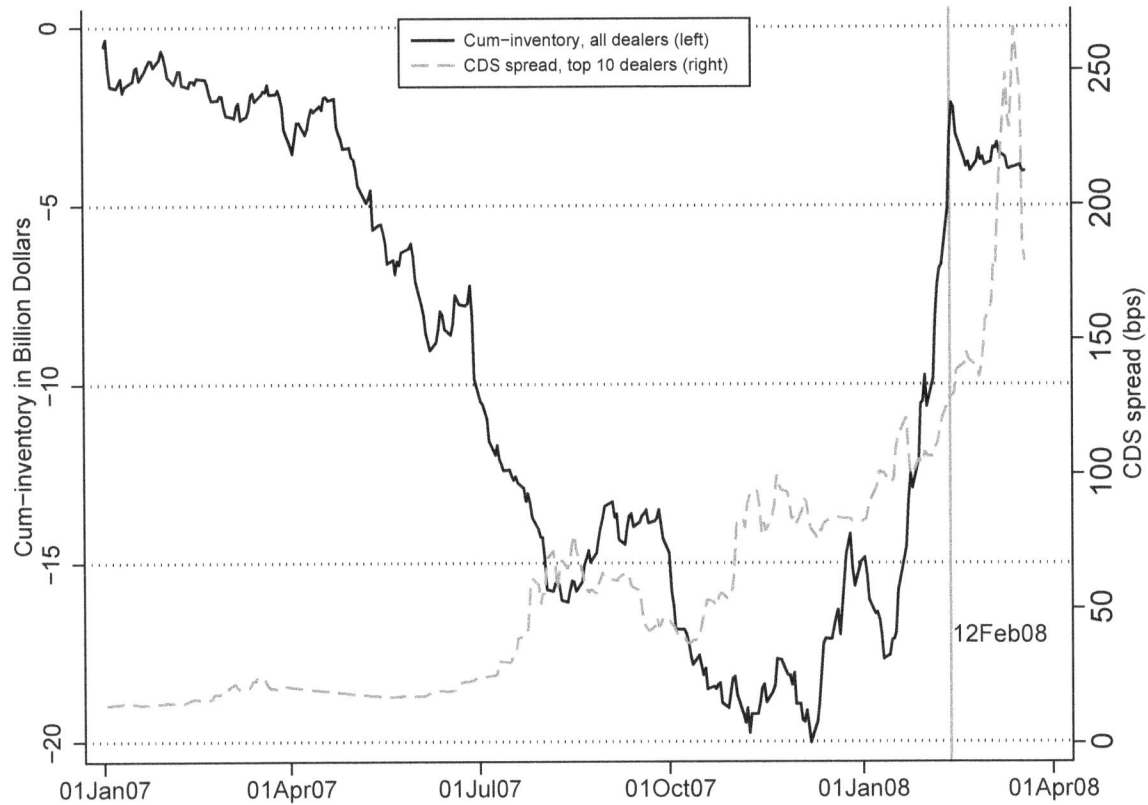

www.ingramcontent.com/pod-product-compliance
Lightning Source LLC
Chambersburg PA
CBHW081619170526
45166CB00009B/3027